MW00935779

DELIVERING MARKETING JOY!

How to Grow Your Business with Promotional Products

KIRBY HASSEMAN

CONTENTS

ACKNOWLEDGMENTS

The journey of writing any book has a lot of bumps and detours. In order make it through this winding road, you always need a lot of help. I can say that was certainly true for me! So here is a likely incomplete list of the great people that helped me get this project done! In addition, it's important to update this list as I updated the book

First, thanks to the team at Hasseman Marketing! Libbie, Dustin, Julie Jeff, Chris and Mom! Thanks for providing me help and inspiration. In addition, special thanks to Josh for helping me update the look of the book AND to Sarah Hart (the best intern ever) for helping me create the audio book too!

Thanks so much for the industry buy in from great advocates like Mark Graham, Dana Zezzo, Rory Campbell, Danny Rosin, Rick Greene, Cliff Quicksell, Roger Burnett, Larry Cohen, Chase Thompson, Mark Tipton, Brian Debottis, Bill Petrie and more!

In addition, I want to send sincere thanks to PPAI Leadership including Paul Bellantone and Kim Todora! Their input and assistance with case studies has been invaluable.

Finally, thanks to my lovely family! My mom and dad Christine and Rod Hasseman have been mentors in this industry since early in my life. And thanks to my girls, Skylar, Jade and Amy Hasseman. You always provide me inspiration! To quote Bryan Adams, "Everything I do, I do it for you!"

FOREWARD

Before you read another word, stop what you are doing and put this book down. That's right. Stop reading and take a moment to slowly survey your surroundings.

If you're in your office or workspace you are likely to see an imprinted coffee mug from last year's company party. How about some branded notepads, sticky notes, a backpack or messenger bag, pens and dozens of other branded desk accessories. Did you see a branded promotional memory stick in your computer? What about an engraved photo frame from an incentive trip or maybe a plaque or award commemorating years of service or some other worthy achievement? If you are sitting in your car waiting on an appointment did you see a logoed ice scraper or sun shade? Or maybe a promotional Mp3 player case, phone mount, keychain, flashlight or portable USB car charger. Wait, were those imprinted reusable bottles in both cup holders?

Maybe you're at home in the kitchen. If so, there's a good chance you noticed a refrigerator magnet (or twelve), one or two give-away calendars, emblazoned oven mitts and potholders, can and bottle openers, measuring cups, wine glasses and more.

Now take a look at what you're wearing today. Maybe you have on a logoed shirt with the name of your company, a favorite golf course or a valuable business partner. Or is it a sweater, jacket, t-shirt or hat with the brand of your favorite sports team. The one you received for arriving early at their last home game. Is that a silicon bracelet on your wrist commemorating or promoting a favorite cause or recognizing a donation?– Starting to notice a trend? We haven't even asked about the bathroom with the dozens of promotional products found there from hand sanitizers to pill cases to towels and dispensers. Promotional products are everywhere and the reason is quite simple; promotional products work!

Recent research tells us that:

- 88 percent of consumers recall the advertiser on promotional products
- 85 percent have done business with the advertiser after receiving a promotional item
- 83 percent like promotional products
- 81 percent keep them because they are useful
- 53 percent use promotional products once a week
- 47 percent keep them for more than a year

These outcomes are music to advertiser's ears – and that's just one of the senses promotional products appeal to. Want in on a little secret? Promotional products are the only advertising medium that can reach all five senses. Want to add sound in your message? There are speakers and ear buds and CD's and mp3 players that can easily fit the bill. Looking to entice the taste buds? Food items are one of the fastest growing categories of promotional items – and they're not just for the holidays. There are literally hundreds of items that will generate an aroma of success, thousands that appeal to a sense of touch (ever tried to put down a Rubik's cube or Slinky) and hundreds of thousands of products that keep brands up front and in focus.

While other traditional media might appeal to one or maybe two of the five senses, only promotional products appeal to a sixth sense – the sense of pride, ownership and appreciation.

Think about it; when was the last time you said thank you to a company for a repetitive TV commercial, or thanked a publisher for another ad in a magazine or waited in anticipation of yet another pop-up ad or video commercial as you navigate the web. Likely you haven't.

Promotional products generate interest, action and loyalty-- distinguishing them as one of the most effective longest lasting and best-loved advertising media in the world. In fact, eight in ten consumers own a promotional product; with 59 percent having a more favorable impression of the brand and 85 percent doing business with the brand after receiving a promotional product.

Now that you have a solid understanding of the power of promotional products, you can continue your journey to Delivering Marketing Joy. But before you do, I want to take a minute to thank the author of this book, Kirby Hasseman, for inviting me to share such rich and compelling information with you.

As president of Promotional Products Association International (PPAI) I am well aware of the many options available for you to purchase promotional products for your business. I also know the value of working with true marketing professionals exponentially increases your chances of marketing success. Kirby and the team at Hasseman Marketing have been delivering marketing joy for over 15 years. You are in very good hands.

1Promotional Products Association International: The Influence of Promotional Products on Consumer Behavior, 2012

Paul Bellantone, CAE
President & CEO
Promotional Products Association International
Direct: 972-258-3050
www.ppai.org

INTRODUCTION...
GIVE YOUR WAY TO SUCCESS!

Breaking news: An historical change is upon us.

No it is not the Rise of the Planet of the Apes (wow that movie was bad). It is a cultural shift in the way business is done. It is happening now. And if you are a fan of doing things "the right way" then you should be excited for the future.

The change has been coming for some time. For years, companies have worked to automate all of their "service" services. They have consistently tried to cut costs with outsourcing phone centers, one size fits all websites or even getting rid of human contact all together. We have all experienced it at one time or another. We have spent endless time on hold coming to the realization that customer service really had nothing to do with the customer at all. Maddening.

From a marketing standpoint, the change has been coming as well. We have lived in an age of "push" marketing forever... since the beginning of time. But the internet--and social networks--is changing that. Right now. Now, more than ever, the customer has a voice. The customer has clout and power. And the customer wants better. We want better.

So the shift is beginning. Companies are beginning to understand that they need to humanize. They need to engage. They need to provide value. They need to GIVE before they ask. What this means is that this large world is becoming small again. Each customer needs to be treated as if we are business owners in a small town! We might see them again in the grocery store. If we treat them badly, they can tell their friends. So as businesses we need to re-visit service and marketing.

We need to GIVE first. We need to work at providing value to our customers so they trust us. We need to think "small" things first.

That's great news...if you want to do things the right way to begin with! As you will read in this book, promotional products provide an amazing way to "give" first to your customers and prospects. These products have the power to help you create real and lasting bonds with your customers. And as you know, by creating real and lasting bonds you build a business that lasts and lasts.

Congratulations. Viva la revolucion! Join it! Give Your Way to Success...by Delivering Marketing Joy!

1

WHAT IS MARKETING JOY?

As you start this book, you might be asking yourself, "What is Marketing Joy?" You might think, "I like the sound of it, but how do I deliver it?"

Imagine the process of creating a fun and creative Trade Show experience. You have worked with your team to come up with a unique theme. You have created a buzz in your industry about your company's offerings and you have invited people to join you at the show. You have created an atmosphere that show participants are interested in. Now you and your team are at the Trade Show and the masses come barreling in! They show you the postcard you sent them in advance of the show. They are bringing peers back to see the demo and get information. They are smiling as they receive their show promo! And now you see them nodding to your team as they "get it." Your booth is a hit! Your traffic is up! You and your team are making sales, or appointments right there at the show!

BOOM! That is Marketing Joy!

During the process of creating that show you realize you want the team to look energized and together. So you order a hip and fun "team uniform" with your logo. The box comes in well in advance of the show. You rush up to open the box and see the shirts look great! You call out to your peers to show off the new products excited about the new opportunity!

BOOM! That is Marketing Joy!

You have created on Social campaign to increase "followers" and to humanize your brand. In doing so, you create a fun campaign and get the staff and customers involved. It's fun and yes, you are promoting the company!

Marketing Joy!

The fact is, Marketing Joy is what happens when you have created a thoughtful, (sometimes) fun, creative marketing campaign and it drives business WHILE making you and your customer smile! Simple as that!

You are adding value to your customer—and bringing them joy—while driving revenue to your company! Think of it as the Law of Attractions for advertising: If you push out good... you get it back!

Or as I simply say, when done right, Marketing Joy is that "Little piece of Christmas morning you get when you (or your customer) open that campaign done just right."

Now you might be thinking this is just a concept full of positive thinking and platitudes. You would be wrong. This is for real. It's based on over 40 years of research, studies and case studies.

And my guess is you already know this. You know it because it is EXACTLY how YOU want to be treated as a customer! You want to do business with companies and organizations that value you! You want to be appreciated. At the very least you don't want to be shown disdain. Right?

Mark Twain said something to the effect of, "I don't know why they call it common sense. It doesn't seem very common!" Unfortunately that statement still rings true. But that's the cool thing about creating marketing joy. The premise is based on common sense AND it is backed up with data.

Marketing Joy is the best kind of win-win marketing campaign and it can be done in nearly any advertising venue. It's about giving your way to success and sales. And that is often best done with promotional products!

So if you are a business owner, entrepreneur, marketer or organizational leader that wonders if something like "marketing joy" could exist, this concept (and this book) is for you.

Let's start with whether or not "marketing joy" is actually real. *(Hint...it is)*.

2

DELIVERING MARKETING JOY...IT IS FOR REAL

It has become an "in thing" these days to take shots at the promotional products industry. Respected business people, legislatures and writers have recently questioned the necessity for these items. There have been proposed laws decreasing the amount that can be spent on these items (a $20 billion industry, and counting) and "controversies" questioning their place in budgets. Mark Cuban (who I love) even wrote that startups should never invest "in swag."

It's all poppycock. (And I say that not just because it's fun to say "poppycock." It's also true!)

The fact is Promotional Products are a proven advertising medium. They work. The best part is, more and more studies are not only showing they work. These studies are showing they work more effectively than other advertising channels. Organizations that want to promote themselves should be looking to spend MORE of their advertising buy on promotional products...not less.

WHAT'S IN A NAME?

I can hear the skeptics now. "You don't need tchotchkes, or trinkets and trash. Those are a waste of money."

These demeaning names piss me off. Forget the fact that these people discredit what I choose to do for a living. That's their prerogative. What bugs me is that it affects their effectiveness.

So let's start with the name. First up, stop calling them crap and maybe you will stop choosing crap. When you stop choosing crap, these products might represent your brand better. Some of my best clients have taken to calling them "premiums." That's great because it changes the way you brand yourself on these items. Let's face it, the products you choose say a lot about your company.

So by taking a little more care in what you put your brand on, you will immediately have better luck with products that affect behavior.

DO THEY WORK?

I am sure every form of advertising is accused of "not working." As I heard once, "Just because you can't put the ball in the basket, doesn't mean there's a problem with basketball. Maybe you're just not good at it."

Promotional Products do work. Many of us have known this for years. But more studies are coming out all of the time that proves it. That's the best thing about marketers getting more interested in measuring ROI. We are getting facts to back up the theory. Here are just a few from a study released in 2010:

- Of 1000 people surveyed that had received a promotional product, 89% could recall the advertiser. Say that out loud people. The name of the game in advertising is to create customer recall. Nearly 90% is a number that you might want to know when you are figuring your budget.
- 14.7% of participants reported contacting the advertiser after receiving the promotional product. That is nearly 3 times greater than other media.

When done right, promotional products are incredibly effective. The more the facts stack up, it's just hard to argue.

WORK TOO WELL?

The great irony is that it can be argued these products work too well. Don't believe me? Well look no further than the laws written to limit the amount of promotional materials that can be given in the healthcare industry to Doctors. These laws were put in place because Big Pharmaceutical companies were creating "undue influence" over these Physicians. Now some will argue that these laws were put in place because of free trips, game tickets, and extravagant dinners.

Maybe so.

But then why legislate the kinds of products that can be given to doctors' offices? To put it simply, these laws were created because promotional products were having a huge influence on healthcare decisions.

The goal of any marketing campaign is to affect behavior change. When you can implement a campaign so effective that it needs to be legislated...you may want to consider that strategy to promote your organization!

Promotional products have been around since the late 1800's and I think sometimes this is part of the reason the results are discounted. Everyone wants to know the newest, hottest ways to reach customers. You should!

But don't sleep on the power of promotional products. Now more than ever, you need to include them in your marketing mix.

In this book, I will spend the time to prove that if you decide to dismiss this entire category you have missed the boat. I will also spend time showing you ways the use each category within this vast marketing medium to grow and promote your business (regardless of what your business is). To top all of this off, I will work with industry pros to give you case studies on how companies have created very real Return On Investment (ROI) on promotional campaigns...and how you can too!

So now that we know it's for real...let's dig in!

3

WHY PROMOTIONAL PRODUCTS WORK

"Let's get more customers. Let's get better customers. Let's spend less money to do so."

This is the battle cry of any business owner, marketer or sales person. Whether you are Vice President of Sales for a Fortune 100 company, or a small business owner in Middle America, the goal is still the same. You want to drive more customers into your funnel. Then once you have them there...you want to keep them!

And of course if you are this VP of Sales or anyone else who is charged with marketing their company, you also understand that there are a LOT of ways to advertise and market your company (or product or service). Between radio, newspaper, magazines, television and the internet, each of these media is working to show you why their way is the best to reach your potential clients. And let's face it... sometimes they might be right.

A mistake some business marketers make is to focus solely on these mass media advertising elements when marketing their company. Though they may utilize promotional products in some cases, these dollars are spent only after the "real" advertising is done. Though many savvy business marketers are really beginning to understand the power of the promotional product, many are still utilizing them like "trinkets and trash."

If you consider this promotional tool this way, those are the kind of results you will get.

In today's marketing mix, well utilized promotional product campaigns can bring powerful, measurable results. But why do these imprinted items bring positive results? And more importantly to you, how can you utilize them to create real results in your marketing plan? That's what we will show you in this book.

First let's talk about why promotional products work. There are many reasons for the many different situations, but let's focus on three simple reasons why they are effect.

Promotional Products are targeted!

Promotional Products are cost effective per impression!

Humans appreciate receiving valuable gifts!

Let's elaborate just a bit.

Promotional Products are Targeted – This is one of the oldest reasons to utilize Promotional Products...and still a viable one. Done correctly, you are giving your promotional product (whatever that product might be) directly to the customer or potential customer. You are reaching out into their office, kitchen, car or yard and greeting them with your "who, what, where" message! As one of my first teachers told me, you are taking your business card and putting it on their wall (or desk or pocket). Since you are reaching directly to the people you want reach, there is little or no waste.

That same teacher handed me a calendar and asked me, "What is the worst thing that can happen to this when you give it to a client?"

I looked over the calendar for a moment, turned and cavalierly threw it in the waste basket. I waited for him to be upset, but he simply laughed and said, "Exactly!"

Smiling at the confused look on my face he explained, "You looked at the calendar—the advertising message—considered it and then discarded it. That's the worst thing that can happen. But consider this; that is the BEST thing that can happen to nearly all other kinds of advertising! If someone listens or sees an ad long enough to consider it, that ad has succeeded. But with our advertising that is your worst case scenario! Most likely that calendar will be hanged and give you valuable advertising space on the customer's wall all year."

Which leads nicely into...

Promotional Products are Cost Effective – When considering many advertising venues you will hear terms like range, frequency, circulation to showcase the overall power or effectiveness of the medium. And although those can be impressive statistics, they are not always totally accurate. Just because 100,000 people CAN listen to a radio station doesn't mean they DO.

When measuring the effectiveness of a well-executed promotional product campaign, I like to consider the CPI or Cost Per Impression of an item. Measuring the CPI of an item gives you a stronger understanding about the power of an individual product. It also quantifies the value to you, the marketing professional, of that same product.

Let's take a promotional watch for example. A decent watch for a customer might cost you $20 (less or more but let's go with this for this example; you can do the math for other price ranges). Initially $20 might sound like a lot to reach this customer. But consider that the average person looks at their watch about twice per hour, 10 hours per day. Let's also assume they wear this watch for the better part of year, or 300 days. That customer has now looked at your branding message 20 times per day for 300 days...or 6000 times! Now if you divide that $20 watch by the 6000 times your branding message was in front of your customer you realize the CPI on this watch was $.0033 per impression! Not a bad investment for your marketing dollar!

Of course you can easily think through the math on any promotional item. You don't need to know any fancy statistics; common sense will do the trick. That's why some of the classic staples of the promotional products industry are products that have lasting power. The more long term usefulness a product has the more value it has to your brand!

Humans Appreciate Receiving Valuable Gifts – Though this sounds like sort of the "duh" moment of the book, it's deeper than that too. It is true that many people like to receive things that are free. Unfortunately sometimes that leads us to think of the lowest common denominator of mooch out there that only comes to trade shows for the free stuff. Those folks are out there...but that is not what I am talking about.

Studies show that giving your customers (or potential customers) a promotional "gift," you actually create a sense of obligation in that person to do business with you. That's right. It's called the Rule of Reciprocity. Studies prove that by giving that $5 item, your customer will actually feel like they owe you or your company the opportunity to do business. You have provided them something of value. Interestingly enough, this Rule states that this effect increases over time. So the more often you present that prospect with a promotional "gift" the more likely they are to give you an order. They subconsciously feel like they owe you!

And though that might not "exactly" be the intention, it is a wonderful added benefit.

I make it a habit. Each time I go to visit one of my customers; I make sure I bring "goodies." As I tell them, I don't want them to say, "Oh no, Kirby is coming." I want them to be excited for my visit saying, "Oh, Kirby is coming! I wonder what he will bring me!" I am NOT above gift giving to gain business. I will trade a $5 promotional item for $1000 worth of business every day!

So remember...promotional products work for three simple reasons. They are a very targeted form of advertising, they are cost effective and people love free stuff (the Rule of Reciprocity)!

If you want to get more customers, get better customers and spend less money doing it, then a well-thought out promotional product strategy had better be a part of your marketing mix!

The key here is "well-thought out" plan. If you simply go around handing out things with your logo to anyone and everyone, you have lost the idea of "targeted." So in essence, you negate one of the things that make promotional products effective. Think about it...have you done that? Then you say, "Wow I didn't get any return on that." Of course you didn't! You blew it!

That's the next step. We are going to work to show you how to use promotional products, where to use them, and hopefully give you thoughts on what targeted marketing pieces might work best for your business.

So let's get started!

4

CUSTOMER RETENTION WITH MARKETING JOY

Let's start with a statistic that should really make you think. Studies show that 69% of customers that leave you (as a customer, donor, supporter, etc.) will do so because of "perceived indifference." They will leave you because they simply don't think you care. Seriously, think about that. Nearly 7 out of ten lost customers come down to the fact that you didn't show them that you gave a crap about them.

This statistic both frightens and excites me.

On one hand, it means that my customers could leave me because I have just been careless and lazy. It means that if I am not careful, my competitors could swoop in and take my revenue...just by caring more! Am I doing enough to show customers (regularly) that I do sincerely appreciate their business? Are you? That can be scary.

On the other hand, it is an entirely fixable (and improvable) situation. If I am not doing enough to show them, I can fix it! It is totally within my power to do so. That's a good thing. I don't have to wait for some cosmic shift in the economy, or some other outside force to change. I can do it all by myself. I just need to care more!

On the third hand (is that even possible?) I see this as an opportunity. It means likely that most businesses are NOT caring enough about their current customers. That means I (and now you) can create systems that allow you to gain market share...through caring!

How cool is that?

So how do we do it? Let's talk about some very concrete ways to make sure your customers know they are appreciated.

SEND CARDS

It's funny. Sometimes the things that make a big difference in your customer's eyes are the simplest. Send your customers a card on their birthday. Send them thank you cards for their business. Send them a holiday card. Send them a Thanksgiving card. Most people open their mail standing over the trash can, because all we get are bills and junk mail. A heartfelt thank you card really stands out.

The reason most people don't send out cards regularly is they lack a system. Let's face it; most of us have good intentions. But those intentions go out the window when we can't find the right kind of card, or we can't find a stamp, or we don't have the person's address. We need to schedule a specific time each day (or week) that we send out cards.

One of my favorite practices is to try to create a reason to send out at least one thank you card each day. Sometimes it will be for a purchase that a customer made. Sometimes it will be just because someone helped you. It's a fantastic practice.

Two things will happen. First, your customers will NEVER think you don't appreciate them. And second, you will have a better attitude about life. If you spend every day trying to find something to be thankful for—guess what—you will become more grateful. That's not a bad side benefit for doing something to help you increase your business!

QUARTERLY THANK YOU PROGRAM

If you are like most businesses, you have 20% of your customers or clients that produce 80% of your sales. It's not a universal rule, but it is surprising how often it is true. So those 20% are the clients you REALLY want to show that you care. So in addition to sending them a birthday card, a

Thanksgiving card and thank you cards, you want to reach out and "touch" them at least once a quarter.

So establish yourself a budget. How much are you willing to spend over the course of a year in order to say "thank you" to these top clients? Remember, these are your bread and butter. This is probably not the time to go cheap. This number will be different for every business, but in my experience, you don't have to break the bank.

Got it?

Now just for argument sake, let's assume this number is $100 per year. You are willing to spend $100 over the course of a year to say thank you to these top clients. Now just divide that number by 4. So you have $25 per quarter to get some sort of gift to give to these clients. This is more than just a gesture. This promotional gift will not only show your appreciation for them. It will also showcase your logo and remind them each and every time they use the gift that you are a great company to work with!

Now just tailor the gifts to your audience. You are now touching these clients 4 more times a year with a great tangible piece of appreciation.

How does this work? Let's give you an example. Let's say you are an insurance agent that has a wide variety of customers. You have business professionals, farmers, families and more. This diverse group of customers gives you an idea of things you do and don't want to give.

So your quarterly gifts might look like this:*

QUARTER 1: ROADSIDE SAFETY FLASHLIGHT.

This makes sense because you are not only promoting your brand, but you are showing you care about your client on the road.

*Product suppliers and item numbers available on page XXX

QUARTER 2: HIGH END TRAVEL MUG AND COOLER BAG.

This is a cool combo because your clients might be thinking of vacations or road trips for the warmer months. This is a great way to remind them that you are with them through the miles and smiles!

QUARTER 3: BBQ SET.

At this point they will be in barbecue season with tailgating just around the corner.

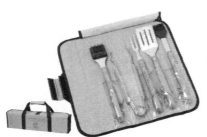

QUARTER 4: EXECUTIVE CALENDAR AND TUMBLER.

These two gifts are sure to stand out in the office and the home.

Obviously these are just a few ideas to get you thinking. There are thousands and thousands of options. But these are some cool things that transcend generations and gender.

*Also, here's a quick tip to make this easier for you. Get with your promotional products consultant and tell them your plans. Then see if you can order all of these at once. Ask to see if they will ship them about a month before you need them. This will allow you to budget a bit. And it will "poof" create a reminder system so you remember it's time to say "thanks" again to your clients. When the boxes arrive it's time to start!

There are lots of ways to thank your clients. These are just two. Feel free to get creative and have some fun thanking your customers. You will be glad you did!

CASE STUDY: THE TEDDY BEAR AND THE CAR DEALER

This case study has been supplied by our supplier partner Vitronic Promotional. This is a great example of how showing you understand and appreciation your customers can help to grow your business! Regardless of your industry, how can you implement a similar idea?

ABC Auto owns eight dealerships throughout the Tri-County area and purchased 600 of item CTG900 Baby Bear by Gund. They bears were evenly distributed to each dealership to use in the service department. Every vehicle in for service with a baby seat got a bear placed in the seat proudly wearing a shirt displaying the dealer's logo.

The results have been phenomenal! The dealerships have received numerous calls of gratitude from the customers and best of all, repeat customer rates have increased! 80% of the bears went to customers in for a routine maintenance check. Of those, 68% have returned for the next visit ON TIME for PRIOR to scheduled! This is a significant increase...all because of the loyalty created from one little teddy bear!

5

THE THREE R'S OF BUSINESS

When it comes to a successful education, old timers will tell us about the 3R's of education. The idea is that a focus on "Readin, wRitin, and aRithmatic" would help create a good student. And though that is hopefully not the entire focus of our education system today, we know that those are the basics for success.

When it comes to business, there are also the THREE "R's" that are a great piece of any successful, long term business. We have already spent an entire chapter on one of the R's— Retention. So let's talk about the other Two R's in a great business! Those are:

1. Repeat Customers

2. Referrals

REPEAT CUSTOMERS

All successful business owners want to have a steady stream of repeat customers that come to our door. These repeat customers are the backbone of any vibrant business. They are the "holy grail." These customers come back again and again and (hopefully) have a loyalty to spending their time and money with us!

They are also our best source for the other R—Referrals—but I will get to that in a minute.

These repeat customers are so great because we have already won them. It takes a great deal of time, energy and money to capture a customer. In fact, it's much harder to convert a non-customer into a customer than it is to sell to a current customer. Depending on which study you believe, it costs 6 to 7 times more to capture a new customer than to sell to a current customer.

It's one of the main mistakes I think many businesses make. We spend most of our time and money on the clients that are hardest to reach!

So we have a base of repeat customers. Great! Now what do we do with them? I think it's safe to say the goal is to grow that base. But how?

The first way is to get these repeat customers to come and do business with us more often! If we can increase the number of times these customers do business with us, we increase sales. Duh...right?

Well in two separate studies (in 1993 and 1994 respectively) promotional products were shown to improve repeat business.

STUDY ONE—FOOD DELIVERY SERVICE

In this study, conducted by Southern Methodist University, 900 people were divided equally into 9 groups. These nine groups were broken down by type of customer (existing residential, new residential, and business customer) and what they received (promotional product, coupon, or nothing). The promotional products and coupons were both valued at $2.

- Customers who received promotional products ordered up to 18% sooner than those who received coupons!

- Customers who received promotional products also averaged up to 18% more orders than those receiving coupons.

In other words, the customers that received the promotional products ordered more quickly and more often than those that received coupons...or nothing.

STUDY TWO—DRY CLEANER

This study, also conducted by Southern Methodist University, tracked the activity of 300 new customers at two locations of a dry cleaner. These customers were randomly assigned one of three groups, all of who received a welcome letter. Two of these groups received, in addition to the letter, a promotional product or a coupon—both valued at $5.

- Over an 8 month period, new customers that received a promotional product spent 27% more than those who received coupons, and 139% more than those who received only a welcome letter.

- Promotional products recipients were 49% more likely than coupon recipients and 75% more likely than letter recipients to patronize the dry cleaner in each of the eight months studied.

Again, those that received promotional products spent more and were more regular customers than those that did not.

If repeat customers are the "Holy Grail" to business success, then you need to consider how cementing that relationship with a promotional product can help you grow.

REFERRALS

Another huge part of any successful business is the second R... referrals. As a business friend once told me, "The best way to get referrals is to deserve them!" That is so true! But I am going to assume that you are running a business that is worthy of referrals. Now let's talk about how to get more of them!

As I mentioned earlier, your current customer base is often the best place to look for growth in your business. It's also the place that many business owners and marketers ignore. Let's face it, your current client base already "gets" you. They understand what you are all about. So they can be a fantastic source of other potential customers.

The problem with referrals is, no really likes to ask for them! Admit it. You don't like asking. Most people don't. Nearly every time I speak to a group, everyone agrees that getting referrals is a great way to grow your business. And just as consistently, most groups admit to failing to "consistently ask" for referrals. See the problem?

How do we make it easier? Give a promotional gift before asking for the referral.

A study done in 1993 by Baylor University shows that customers who receive a promotional product are more willing to provide referrals than those that don't. The study was conducted with 20 Mary Kay beauty consultants, half of whom distributed a promotional gift to customers; the other 10 offered no promotional gift. The results were impressive.

- Customers who received a promotional product were 14% more likely to provide leads than those that did not.
- Salespeople who gave promotional products to their customers received 22% more referrals than the salespeople who did not use the promotional gift.

Providing even a small promotional gift to customers will increase the likelihood that they will provide you with great referrals. Combine that with the fact that you have a business worth referring...and you have business gold!

CREATE A REFERRAL PROGRAM

Are you still struggling to ask for that referral? What about creating a program that asks for you? It would go something like this:

Create a flyer that could be emailed, mailed, faxed (sent via smoke signal) to your current customer base. This flyer would advertise a nice "Referral Gift." This gift could be anything from a nice watch to a piece of luggage (use your imagination). The gift does not have to break the bank, but it does need to be nice enough to garner attention.

Send the flyer letting customers know that if they provide a referral that turns into business for you, they will receive this fabulous gift. Boom.

Here are some things to consider on a referral program.

1. The gift needs to be nice enough to get your customer to act.

2. Make the first purchase minimum enough that the proceeds from that sale will cover the cost of the item. That way you might break even on this transaction, but now you have a customer for life!

3. Make it feel somehow "exclusive." Maybe you only send it out in groups to your top 20% of clients. They are the most likely to give you the best referrals anyway!

This simple program will take "the ask" out of the referral! You have gone from asking them for a referral to giving them an opportunity for a great gift!

Either way, you want to have a strong case of the Three R's if you want a successful business. Now you know how promotional products can help you!

6

GROWING YOUR BUSINESS WITH TARGET ACCOUNTS

At this point in the book, you might be saying, "Okay I get that you need to retain customers. I understand you need to grow within your current client base. But at some point you need to get new customers to grow as well.

You're right.

So let's focus on that now...with Target Accounts. I think this is one of the most powerful ways to grow your business. Promotional products are most effectively used when they are targeted. That is why this concept works so well. Let's start with the concept.

First, you want to create your "target" list. I have also heard this referred to as the Dream list, Bullseye List, and Bucket List. Regardless of the name, you want to create the list of 100 perfect prospects for your company. These are the exact kinds of clients you want to do business with. I base this list on a number of factors. They include proximity, kinds of businesses, reputation for payment, culture and more. You are going to know the factors that are important for your ideal customer. This is the kind of customer where successfully getting just one of them, will quickly affect your sales numbers!

This is a powerful step for a couple of reasons. First, as I just said, this Target Customer is the kind who can REALLY impact your sales. They have the wherewithal to purchase what you are selling...in big numbers. Second, it is MUCH more cost effective to market to 100 people than it is 10,000! You can be much more personal, targeted, and relentless!

Now, DO take the time to get them on paper (or in your CRM if you use one). When getting them recorded, make sure to include all the pertinent contact information. This will keep you from "creating reasons" not to follow up. You will have all the information at your fingertips...so no reason not to call!

By the way, this first step is a huge one. Take some time and don't skimp on the information. You will be glad you have it right in the long run.

Now that you have your list it's time to create your plan. I recommend breaking your Target list of 100 into more manageable numbers, like 5 or ten at a time. This does a couple things. First, by breaking the numbers down, you make the list more reasonable to follow up with. In addition, once you have gone through the first 5 (all the way through the process) you have your next 5 all ready to go. You will be glad you did. On more than one occasion I have made the list of only 5, and then when I got through it, got stalled because I had to start the "target list" all over.

Once you have the Target List created, it's time to make the impact with these great potential customers with promotional products! Now it's time to have some fun.

If you have chosen wisely (and in this case, I mean big!) you will need to understand that these are clients that most people would want! So they probably have "everyone" marketing and selling to them. That's the bad news. The good news is, most people are being lazy when reaching out. They are sending letters, or cold calling or some other "shot in the dark" sales technique.

Since you don't want to blend in with the other wannabes, you need to create a creative campaign that will stand out. I recommend a "three tier" campaign that. This means you will send 3 creative mailers—one after another—until the follow up.

But you really need to stand out here. Don't just send a letter. If you want fantastic results, you need to set out to make a fantastic impact. Let's go through a fictitious example:

Let's say my friend Bill has a Home Improvement store that focuses on carpet and paint. Though he certainly wants every "do it yourselfer" to think of him, he can make larger sales AND repeat sales if he focuses his marketing efforts on contractors. They are in the market for his products over and over. So Bill might make his Target List starting with contractors he wants to do business with.

This is when the project can really be fun. Here are some ideas for mailers that he might send:

Mailer 1: He sends a box with a nice measuring tape with his stores logo and phone number on it. It would need to be a nice one if he is sending it to a contractor. They won't appreciate junk on something like that! With the measuring tape he might include a letter asking if their current supplier is "measuring up" on service and price. He might include other verbiage about having "room for growth," and their specialty being the "height of service." You get the idea. Have some fun to tie the letter to the item.

Mailer 2: In the second mailer, Bill might send a Giant Pencil. This is really designed to get his attention and make them smile. The letter might include something about "penciling him in for a meeting" or "having trouble finding time to source carpet." You really want to get the clients raising eyebrows here.

Mailer 3: Finally he might send a nice travel mug with an offer to buy him a cup of coffee. In the letter, explain how you know they are "on the go" and you respect their time. Bill might also promise to keep the business relationship "hot" by giving leads back to the contractor. Then it's time to let the prospect know that Bill will be following up (if they haven't called already).

Now you might be thinking, "Wow! This is a lot of money to throw at one prospect." And you are right. This is probably $40 to $50 per prospect here. But you also need to remember that these are clients that can spend thousands and thousands each and every year. So their impact can be well worth it. It's also worth noting that you are not going to spend this much chasing each customer...just the Target list!

Now the procedure becomes simple.

First, choose your 3 to 5 first Target Accounts. (Make it a number you KNOW you can follow up with). I tend to choose them based on the ones I am most excited about working with the soonest. This will give me the most motivation to get this process rolling.

Second, once you have chosen the Targets, send out the mailers. I tend to space them out a week apart. This is a bit of a long sales cycle. But it ensures that they will have time to digest the message, even if they are out on vacation, business travel, etc.

Third, just like any business process, the fortune is in the follow up! You must work the phones now to get your appointments with the Target List. If you have done these mailers right (and been creative) you will have a great deal of success. Be bull-headed in your follow up though. You have invested a lot of money on these prospects! Work hard to get some time in front them now!

If you have chosen wisely on your promotional items and your themes, you will not only have made an immediate impact with your Target list, but you will also have the chance to have long term advertising with them as well!

CASE STUDY FROM BRANDFUEL

Fellow Marketer (and owner of BrandFuel) Danny Rosin shared this compelling Case Study. They worked with a sales organization to create a targeted campaign to grow sales. Though the organization did not want to share exact numbers, they did agree that the numbers were VERY close to these projections!

Custom FuelKits for Marketing, Sales, Human Resources & Membership Programs

Would you rather have a salesperson grab a pen to give away, or have her present a FuelKit to the prospect?

Sales Case Study:

Sales people: 89 | **Kit cost (with freight):** $19

89 sales reps each make 10 new prospecting cells

89 x 10 x $19 = $16,910 investment expense for 890 kits

Anticipated close percentage on 890 kits delivered to prospects - 4% or 36 new clients

Average Annual Sale - $20,000

Profit per annual sales per client = $8,000

$8,000 annual profit per new client x 36 sales - $288,000 gross profit

Return on investment: $288,000 gross profit

$16,910 investment expense = *$271,090 net profit*

7

MARKETING JOY FOR TRADE SHOW SUCCESS

Tell me...has this ever happened to you? You (or your boss, or your assistant, or someone) realize there is a trade show coming up. Then someone in the organization says "We need to get some crap to hand out at this show!" My guess is you have heard it, or said it. Don't be ashamed.

The problem of course is that if your entire strategy to a trade show is "we need to get some crap," then your results were probably equally crappy! So let us show you the way to have an actual plan...and get the most out of your next exhibit!

PRE-SHOW

When it is at all possible, get a list of everyone that has confirmed to come to the show. Though a lot of trade shows probably have a list of last minute sign ups, they will likely have a great list of attendees that are registered and ready to attend. They are likely making preparations (and if they are smart) creating a strategy for working the show themselves. Get that list! As a matter of fact, I have a couple of clients that will not do a show if the organizers won't provide a list. Now that you have it...

Step 1: Send each attendee an email inviting them to come to your booth!

Your best bet would be to be as creative as possible. Try to wet their whistle as to why they need to come and see you. Do you have a great promotional item? Do you have a fun theme? Are you giving free beer? Whatever. Let them know that you want them to come and see you, where your booth is located, and why they should look for you! Depending on how long you have until the show, you might even reach out more than once!

Step 2: Send a direct mail piece to mirror the email.

Make this direct mail piece match the theme of the booth. I like this direct mail piece to be either a postcard (so they don't have to open it to see it) or a personal card. The more impactful the direct mail piece, the better the attendance at the booth!

AT THE TRADE SHOW

As a side note, a quick tip for a trade show is to have people who know the product or service and are comfortable selling at the booth. A lot of the time a company will put warm bodies at the booth that don't know the sales process. This detracts from the credibility of the company. So when you are staffing...don't just bring anyone!

Step 3: Have a Theme!

If you want to stand out from the competition in the long rows of Trade Show Masses, think about creating a theme for the show! This not only gives you ammunition for how to dress and what to hand out, it can help with all of your planning for the event.

Step 4: Have a hand out for the masses.

With this you want to have a plan too! Do you want your handout to drive traffic to the booth? Do you want it to have a "lasting impact" after the show? Do you want it to do both? Or do you want it to stay at the bottom of the trade show bag never to come out again? It's up to you...so make sure you actually think out the audience, the item and its impact. Obviously, your promotional consultant can help you think this through. If you don't have one, please let us at Hasseman Marketing know! We would love to help.

Step 5: Have a VIP Gift

Sometimes at a trade show a current customer will stop by the booth. This is a wonderful opportunity to make a big deal about their business and thank them. You also might have leads that you have a connection or show a real interest in your product or service. This is a great time to reach below the table and get out a VIP gift.

You could say "Stan, I really appreciate your business and for taking the time to stop and see me today. I am not giving this to everyone, but please take this as a small token of my appreciation."

Or with a prospect, "Janice I think we are on the same page. I know you have a lot of folks you want to see today, but I really appreciate you taking the time to talk with me. I am not giving these to everyone, but please take this and I will follow up with you after the show."

These VIP gifts would be a nicer gift and you wouldn't need that many of them. But you can really increase the impact with those special contacts by making them feel like the VIP's they are!

AFTER THE SHOW...THE FORTUNE IS IN THE FOLLOW UP!

Step 6: Follow Up Quickly with Email

This is the bare minimum follow up. But have a system in place to follow up with everyone that stopped by the booth. Make sure you thank them for coming and remind them who you are and what you do! These folks have seen a lot of people during that short period of time, so do your best to remind them of you. If you remember the conversation it would be great to reference it! But the sooner you can follow up, the more you portray the sense that you and your company is "on it!"

Step 7: Follow Up with a Card

This can be a really nice personal touch. Now I understand, if there are thousands of people then maybe this is not realistic. If not, then another touch with a direct mail postcard might fit the bill. But this will be one more way to get across their desk and to remind them of your "awesomeness." The personal card, when appropriate can REALLY make you stand out!

If the idea of writing, stamping, and sending all of those thank you notes makes you squeamish, you can look into other automated ways of doing it. At Hasseman Marketing we use a system called Send Out Cards. It's perfect for a personal follow up piece like this one. If you want information on that you can go to www.sendoutcards.com/100300 and see for yourself!

Step 8: Follow Up with a Call

Yes that's right, call them! After going through this process, this is a great way to make the final personal touch. It's time to reel them in!

So that's the 8 step process to making your Trade Shows more effective. Depending on how many emails you send in the email steps you will have touched each prospect between 7 and 12 times. Studies show it takes an average of 7 touches before a prospect buys...so you have done a complete job!

It's not rocket science, but you need to have a plan in order to get the best results!

The coolest part of this chapter is that when I asked for Case Studies, one of the people that responded was a friend and mentor from Halo Branded Solutions, Rick Greene. He sent this to me and I will include it...great minds think alike! Thanks Rick!

TRADE SHOW CASE STORY BY RICK GREENE!

We once had an office-supply equipment manufacturing client complaining, in a general sense, about the lack of trade show traffic at their booth at the 17 trade shows his company exhibited at each year... that every booth looked basically the same and dozens of lookie-loos walked briskly by a bunch of office machines, trying not to make eye-contact. He wanted EVERYONE to stop at and walk into their booth because everyone attending his industry trade shows were potential buyers.

Promotional products are the answer to maximize trade show results. As long as you remember that the LEAST important part of the trade show experience... is the trade show. Pre-Show Marketing and Post-Show Follow Up are the key to getting the attention of and landing new clients. Here is what we did for this customer.

We developed a 'theme' for his booth – and that theme was "It's A Jungle Out There". He sent an invitation to entire attendee pre-registration list to visit their booth. Not an email, not a fax... a hard copy printed invitation with monkey and tiger graphics, jungle colors and little fuzzy animal weepuls with google eyes and ribbon with the booth number on it.

The invitation talked about the vast choice they had in purchasing office equipment, that it was confusing and, indeed, a 'jungle out there'. It was fun, it was brisk and to the point and it included a cute little weepul dude to maximize impact.

At the show itself, we went all out to make their booth a thing of Tarzan-like beauty. We arranged with a local garden nursery to rent some leafy foliage in pots and we lined the booth with them. We populated the 10 x 30 booth with large stuffed animals... lions and tigers and bears (oh, my) and elephants and zebras. They had a counter with smaller animals that potential clients, who met with them for 5 minutes or longer, got. And they gave the BIG ones, the 2 and 3 foot tall ones, every hour on the hour. They were shipped home for the winners so they didn't have to struggle with big stuffed animals on the plane, but if they wanted to take it with them, they could. We had a tape look of exotica music with jungle caws and hoots and native drums playing. The booth staff wore jungle khaki and pith helmets (with the logo on the band). You almost expected the Jungle Cruise boat from Disney World to come around the next bend. Their trade show booth was a fully immersive experience with a cohesive theme that tied into their tag line... It's a Jungle Out There, folks! And the booth was a SHOW STOPPER. Everyone who walked by came in and learned about this company and why their office equipment is different or better than the boring booth across the aisle.

The first event was a SMASH. They came home with 700% more leads than the previous year and they used the jungle theme at every show they did that year, then went with a Baseball theme the following year, which we also helped with. For the baseball theme, we used the tag line "Touch All the Bases" of our service, our quality, our pricing, etc. This time the pre-show invitation was a FOUR PART mailing – first base, second base, third base and home run, each week featuring another aspect of their company and what sets them apart. And they SET APPOINTMENTS with key buyers the second year, making sure to secure meetings with key buyers at large companies BEFORE the show. In just two years, they completely transformed the way they worked their important trade shows and after each show the sales staff was buried with solid leads and orders.

The message is, don't just set out a bowl of stick pens and think you've done your show promos the right way. That's for trick or treaters and won't get you much of a response.

Be creative. Be WILDLY creative and spend some money on pre-show mailings and décor and uniforms and fun, desirable branded merchandise and your trade shows can be productive again instead of a chore or a bore.

ANOTHER TRADE SHOW CASE STUDY

And because Trade Shows are such a big part of the business landscape I thought I would include another great case study here! Thanks to PPAI for contributing this one!

Company Name - Echoserve
Campaign Type -
Trade Shows And Exhibitions
Promotional Keywords -
Developing Trade Show Traffic
Objective -
To increase tradeshow booth traffic and compel key prospects to linger just a little longer in the booth.

Strategy Execution -
At a medical imaging tradeshow, Echoserve tapped into the predominately male demographic by setting up two old-fashioned shoeshine stands. Booth personnel wore shoeshine aprons to reinforce the retro atmosphere. While booth visitors were receiving complimentary shoeshines (from professional shiners), they were presented with a custom-printed newspaper containing news articles that were actually Echoserve's marketing messages. The shoeshine allowed the prospect to sit down for a moment, detach from the din of the tradeshow, catch his breath and learn about Echoserve's products and services and get a free shoeshine, too! On leaving the shoeshine stand, the prospects were presented with logoed shoe polish, the custom "newspaper" and a branded tote bag to carry it.

Results -
Giving the prospects a moment to focus on Echoserve worked. The shoeshine encounter generated 69 leads which, in the year following the show, resulted in $100,000 in new sales.

8

CREATING MARKETING JOY WITH DIRECT MAIL

Gary Vaynerchuk recently said "Marketers ruin everything!" Keep in mind that Vaynerchuk is a marketing guy. But he points out that as soon as marketers find something that works, they (we) tend to use it to death until it becomes a nuisance. Consider email. We used to get excited each and every time we got an email. We read every single one! Now we can't wait to hit the "delete" button so we can get rid of the nuisances.

The same can be true for many forms of Direct Mail. Direct mail is historically a great marketing tool for small businesses. It still can be. The problem is, this is a case where some marketers have ruined it for the rest of us. We know this as consumers.

Where do you open your mail? Many of us answer that question, "Over the trash can." We are standing there (mentally) hitting the delete button on marketers. Tell the truth, you are probably almost stunned these days when you get a real, sincere piece of mail!

So can you do? You can stand out...that's what.

One way you can stand out is to get noticed before you hit the "circular file." To do this, some marketers will create direct mail that looks like a real card. Some will even go to the lengths of having someone hand write out the envelope. This is a good news/bad news proposition. The good news is, handwritten envelopes DO tend to get opened. And if you have a small group you need to send a message to, this is a great way to make sure they see it. The bad news with this tactic is if your customer opens mail thinking they are getting a personal piece of mail, and it's just an ad, it can backfire. You seem disingenuous, and the customer will likely (sometimes subconsciously) resent you and your company for it.

Another obvious way to get your message seen before it hits the trash pile is to scrap the envelope. You can send a colorful postcard or a flyer without putting it in an envelope. I actually like this tactic for some campaigns. But this idea too, has shortcomings. First, you are usually limited to what you can include on the space you have to imprint (especially with a postcard) AND you are never quite sure what condition your marketing pieces is going to arrive in! Again, sometimes this is fine. But sometimes these limitations are just too annoying.

One of the best ways to ensure a successful direct mail campaign is to incorporate promotional products WITH your direct mail. The results of this math equation should really get your attention.

Direct Mail + Promo = Marketing Gold!

But why does this combination work so well? Let's get to it.

GETTING IT OPEN

First and foremost, using a promotional product can help you create what I call "bumpy mail!" Bumpy mail (or dimensional mailers) are packages that are odd shaped or bumpy. This unique shape calls to the customer or prospect "open me!" Curiosity will help you "kill the cat" because your potential client will want to know what is in the package.

But don't just take my word for it! Let's take a look at a study done in 1993. This study, done by Baylor University, sent packages to 3000 school administrators. They were divided into three groups. The first group received an envelope with a sales letter, sales collateral and postage-paid business reply card. The second group received an envelope with similar contents plus a promotional product. The third group received all of the contents listed above, delivered in a box with a die cut slot, or "dimensional package," instead of an envelope.

The results (as you might expect) were impressive.

- Those who received a promotional product in a dimensional package responded at a rate that was 57% higher than those who received the same promotional product in an envelope!

- Response rates for the dimensional package recipients were 75% higher than for the group who received only a sales letter!

In case you were skimming, you might want to read that last line again. *Response rates for the dimensional package recipients were 75% higher! Wow!*

Now I can hear those "Yeah-But" folks now.

"Yeah but the cost of shipping is going to be higher for that piece."

Of course it will be! But how much is a 75% increase in response rates worth to you? Remember a key word here. This is not a 75% increase in OPEN rates. This is RESPONSE rates! If you can't increase your sales (and overcome in the increase in shipping) with that kind of response rate, you need to seriously reconsider your sales offer!

THE LASTING IMPACT

Here's the thing; I think if I ended the chapter with that information it would be enough. But the best part about adding a promotional product to your direct mail is I get to say "But that's not all folks!"

I have always wanted to say that!

The fact is, when you add Promo to your Direct Mail, you get all of the other benefits of promotional products AFTER your customer opens the offer! Remember the chapter on why promotional products work for you? This is the super extra bonus package with direct mail. They still apply here.

1. Remember the Rule of Reciprocity: Customers feel good about you and your company when they receive something from you. By adding something of value to the direct mail offer, you create a sense of value. This creates a better opportunity to sell to this client long term.

2. Totally Targeted: This promotional piece is still super targeted. You have reached directly into this prospects home or office...and are communicating to them there.

3. Lasting Impression: You have now created a long term advertising message (if you chose the product correctly) long after the postcard, letter or flyer has been thrown away.

FIND YOUR WATERMELON

Years ago I was in a sales training seminar with a Promotional Products Industry expert, Cliff Quicksell Jr. He told a story about a young industry professional that needed to get a message to only 6 people. She needed to get it to them...and she needed to make sure they did NOT throw the letter away by mistake.

This young pro, as Cliff tells it, took a Sharpie and wrote the message on six watermelons...and sent them! "She had a tough time with the post office," Cliff said. "But she finally got them to take them.

So I ask you. You come in Monday morning and there is a watermelon on your desk. Do you read it?"

I love that story! The message is clear; Find your watermelon!

While you may not have to send giant fruit (though that would be awesome), you better stand out. And promotional products can help you do that in a cost effective, results-based way!

CASE STUDY WITH HASSEMAN MARKETING

I always tell clients that you can tell what I really believe in by what I put my name (and therefore my money) on! This past year Hasseman Marketing spent our time and money creating what we call our Box Mailer for clients and prospects. The goals of the campaign were to (of course) increase sales, showcase our company as an industry leader, and build goodwill with clients and prospects. The results were tremendous!

Inside the box (which we got for FREE from the United States Postal Service) was a custom made flyer with aggressive deals for promotional items. We also partnered with a small group of our supplier partners to provide samples of a few of the featured items in every box! This accomplished a couple of things.

1. It created our "watermelon." The box was big and likely to be opened anyway. But when you add the "noisy and shaky" nature of the box, it was a sure thing!

2. The goodwill it created was huge! We planned on this being a "marketing" mailer. But each of our sales team got thank you notes, emails and calls about the cool package customers got in the mail! Bonus!

And did we make money? That's the real question right? For this first mailer we spent around $2500 in materials, flyers, products and mailing. We tracked the sale of each item in the flyer. Our sales from the flyer alone were over $17,000.

CASE STUDY WITH CLIFF QUICKSELL JR.

Since I used his story, I thought it would be appropriate that I also included a case study from Cliff here. Thanks to PPAI for letting me use this!

Company Name - Cliff Quicksell & Associates, an iPromoteu Affiliate

Campaign Type - Self-Promotions

Promotional Keywords

Stimulating Sales Meetings
Activating Inactive Accounts
Using Sales Aids for Door Openers

Objective

In a marketing and advertising world cluttered with messaging, the goal was to design a creative marketing piece that would break through the clutter and identify a significant pain point that our prospects were feeling as well seeing that we make a significant point of difference with our marketing efforts. The ultimate goal was to have a door opener that would give the recipient cause to either call or take a call in order to set an appointment to discuss the clients marketing efforts. Each agreed that a 25% appointment rate setting would be the ideal goal.

Strategy Execution

We decided to take a different spin on the typical phrase... "Make sure you're comparing Apples to Apples". As mentioned we wanted to look at us as being different and having the ability to deliver that same point of difference to their marketing efforts. Thus the different message: "When others are comparing Apples to Apples..." (when you open the box) "Be an Orange"..."Let Us Show How We Bring Marketing To Life". Further we identified that marketing must be "...strategic, measurable & creative to be noticed", the principals name was also printed on the collateral along with the phone number and other contact information. Inside the box, we surrounded the orange stress ball with raffia to have it appear as if it we packaged like fruit is normally packaged. To further add dimension, we added an orange air freshener so when the box was opened most of your senses were engaged. The stress ball had the message"Be An Orange" printed on it as well as the distributors name and contact information. This marketing piece was small, compact and affordable. Lastly, the piece was shrink-wrapped in clear film and labeled and posted so when the recipient received the piece it stood out and would be opened immediately.

Results

Results ranged from 40 to 78% appoint rates. Many of the affiliates stated that client conversations were more about marketing effectiveness, driving ROI (Return on Investment) and ROO (Return on Objective) than the typical commodity priced based conversations. A few cases generated projects that exceeded twenty thousand dollars in sales with high profitability.

9

MAKING YOUR EVENT BIG WITH PROMO

Creating and hosting a "slam dunk" event for your company or organization can have a huge impact on your success. Whether it's a fundraiser, an educational event or an open house, a well-run event can help increase loyalty and create revenue.

But just like anything else in business, if you want to have an exceptional event, the devil is in the details.

Obviously this is not an event planning book. There are plenty of those out there. But there are some really cool ways to incorporate premiums to take the event from "fine" to "extra special." I want to outline some of those here and I will do so by taking you through the process of an event we host each year.

CREATE YOUR THEME

Most successful events have some sort of theme to build around. The more fun and creative the theme, the more you can build it up. So spend some time around the brainstorm table and come up with a theme that really moves the needle for your audience.

After you have created the theme, you can take it to the next level by creating an event logo. You don't have to do this, but it helps to brand everything at the event and make it feel "first class." And you don't need to spend big bucks on this. Have a staff contest and come up with something fun and simple! It will help to improve the overall impression of the entire event.

Each year, our company hosts a Customer Appreciation Show. The event has evolved from a strictly "thank you" event for our customers, into a real business event complete with Trade Show set up and a speaker. We want to continue to say "thank you" sincerely to clients. But we also want to provide them a great deal of value for taking time out of their day. We host this event in October each year, not only because it works for our calendar, but also because it is a great time to promote ideas for year-end corporate giving. We choose a different theme to build around each year, and this year our theme was "Oktoberfest."

The best part about coming up with the theme is, the details start to fill in quickly. Once you have the theme you can quickly start talking about food, music, venue and promotions.

In our case we reached out to our vendors (who are showcased at the event) and let them know the theme. Some of the vendors will create giveaways and flyers around the theme. So the more advanced notice we can give them, the better. Of course, the more buy-in you have on the theme, the more unified your event will look. So do your best to get anyone that is outside of your organization to understand the theme as well.

STAFF UNIFORM

The theme also allows you to start thinking about what the staff will wear. If you have staff working the event, you want to have something that will be comfortable for the day. But I also like to have something that stands out. If a customer needs to find someone to help them, I want to make sure it's easy! You don't have to make it a crazy color (though that is fine). You can stand out by just all wearing some sort of logoed apparel that looks sharp...and is the same color. We chose a simple blue this year that was a "newer" style. This allowed us to have a look that wasn't loud, but we knew no one else would be wearing. Simple...but we stood out.

PRE-EVENT PROMOTION

A fun theme can also translate into a fun pre-event marketing piece. Each event will be different, but direct mail can be a very effective way to promote your event in a targeted way. Want to create a piece that reaches the audience but then has staying power? Create a direct mail postcard (with the theme incorporated) and then include a nice magnet built in. This will not only get their attention right in the mailbox (without them having to open anything), but will also give you staying power in their office or their home.

Another way to incorporate premiums would be to combine the promotion with Social Media. You can show, discuss, and tease the premiums that will be available at the event. Going to give away some nice door prizes or other items? Great! Promote that through Social Media. Just showing you will be giving away items at the event will affect human behavior and drive traffic!

AT THE EVENT...FIRST IMPRESSIONS

I know I am dating myself, but I remember a scene from the original Karate Kid movie. Mr. Myagi was teaching Daniel-san to shape the Bonsai trees. He told Daniel-san to close his eyes and imagine what the tree should look like. He told him to see it like a picture. Then he told him to open his eyes and "make the picture."

That's a little like planning an event. Close your eyes and imagine all the details of the event. Now go make the picture.

Here are some quick questions to ask yourself:

1. What do I want people to see first when they come into the event?
2. What do I want them to hear? Smell?
3. Will they see signage with the theme?
4. Do they need signage to direct them to the event?

At our event, we wanted to have them see the enormity of the event, but be welcomed by smiling faces (in event specific shirts!). Our staff then has them sign in (so we can thank them later for coming) and then explains how to enter to win prizes. We also give them a rundown of all that is going on so they are not totally overwhelmed. It's a quick process, but we work hard to make sure their first step into the event is a positive one.

During this time we give them an event bag (remember, this is a bit like a trade show event) so they have something to carry their goodies in. As you would expect, this bag has the event logo and theme on it prominently. In addition, we give them a "game piece" that encourages them to go to all of the vendors. By doing so they get a chance to win valuable prizes! As a side note, these prizes better be good, otherwise no one will do it!

KEEPING THE THEME CONSISTENT

When done right, you really can carry your theme all the way through the event. Create signage for the event that is theme based to give directions, communicate education, or even create a photo op! (Seriously give thought to this! If you can get your attendees to take their picture and post it online for you...GOLD!)

Going to have food at your event? Consider keeping the theme going on your napkins, plates, and cups. Often this does not cost that much more and it makes your event seem well thought out and first class.

FOLLOW UP AFTER THE EVENT

In almost the entire business world, most people fall on their faces in the follow up. So make sure you have an actual plan in place to thank your attendees for coming. Often this can be done with a simple email campaign to recognize that you actually did notice the participants were there. But if you have a few select clients, this might be the place to take it to the next level.

Create a quick mailer with one last premium (with the theme) that goes to your "target list" or your "top clients" or whatever. Just one last touch like this will not only make your event (and your organization) stand out, but it will also provide one more "lasting impact" piece for their desk, office or home.

So go make your next spectacular! Go get it!

EVENT CASE STUDY: SELLING A BUILDING!

I heard this story and felt like I HAD to include it! This one comes from Mark Tipton with Promotional Products Supplier Gold Bond. How about creating an event with promo to sell a building!

A real estate agent in Atlanta had a 10-story office complex that he was trying to sell right about the time the recession began. It sat empty for two years with very little activity at all. It was all he could do to get someone to even look at it.

Then one day he had an idea. What if I created a memorable event by setting up a miniature putt putt hole on each floor of the office building beginning with the first hole." on the 10th floor and working our way down. When they finished the 9 hole course and made their way down to the first floor, he would have a sunglass fitting set up complete with tables of popular, fashionable sunglasses, mirrors, and chairs. To cap off the fun, putt putt tour of the building, each attendee would try on, select, and depart with a cool, new pair of sunglasses.

It worked! Two days after hosting the event and creating a fun, memorable experience for the potential buyers, the building sold! Without a single bite for two years, the building sold in two days after the event!

There is power in promotional products, but when used as a tool to meet a need while also creating an emotional, unique experience, the possibilities are limitless.

10

COMPARING PROMO TO OTHER MEDIA

The fact is, each business owner and marketer have very difficult choices to make when deciding how to market their business. No one I know, or have ever worked with, has unlimited budgets and resources. So you have to be smart and do your best to get the most "bang" for your advertising buck! We all do!

So let's discuss the best use of YOUR advertising dollars.

How? I want to do this by comparing Promotional Products to other forms of advertising.

But before I do, I want to point out my intentions.

It is NOT my intention to take shots at other forms of media. There is a time and a place for all of these advertising forms.

There are lots of different forms of advertising in the world today. Some of these include TV ads, Print Ads, Radio Ads, Online Ads and many more. One of the common themes with all of these is they are Interruption based ad models. In other words, the advertiser is consuming some form of media and the advertiser needs to interrupt that consumption so they can promote their organization, company or product.

This is the model that has been used for hundreds of years. Philosophically, I think Promotional products are different. With the use of Promo, you are providing value on the front end (with lasting impact) in order to gain customers long term. But we have discussed this. What is new?

What is new is how the customer views advertising. The customer agrees with me. But let's not take my word for it. Let's compare the media (much of this is based on a 2009 study released by PPAI).

So first let's establish how marketing and advertising effectiveness is measured.

I have talked before about the "3 R's" of a successful business. I told you that every business wants "Repeats, Retention and Referrals." These "3 R's" are sure to create a long term successful business. It turns out that the best way to measure advertising effectiveness also includes 3 R's.

These 3 R's are Reach, Recall and Reaction!

REACH, RECALL AND REACTION

These 3 R's of advertising are very important to consider. But in my humble opinion, not all R's are created equal!

REACH: How many people do you reach? Obviously this is important...right? Sure it is. You want to reach as many people as you can for the amount of money you spend. The problem with this "R" is that it can be manipulated. Some advertising sales people will point out that 100,000 have access to this channel, or read this paper, or drive by this sign every day!

Wow! Impressive number!

But just because they could listen to the channel, drive by the sign or watch the show doesn't mean they do! And even if they do...did they actually see it? Okay...let's say they did see it. Great! But what you really want is...

RECALL: How many of those people actually recall you and your message? Isn't that one of the real goals of advertising? You want people to remember the ad! Studies show that at any given time about 3% of the population is actually in the market for your particular good or service. That's a small percentage! So when they have decided that they need your help, you want to make damn sure these folks remember you!

But the real holy grail of business success lies in...

REACTION: How many react (in a positive way) to the message. You want to reach them, yes. You want them to remember you, sure. But at the end of the day you want them to pick up the phone and call! You want them to go to their phone and email. You want them to go the website and buy! You (and your business) want a positive reaction!

It's the 3 R's of advertising. Let's see how this study says each advertising media fares. Here is an honest evaluation.

REACH: Let's face it. Reach is the "R" that promotional products are at the disadvantage. When you, as a business owner, invest in a TV spot, you are going to reach more people than with one promotional product. No doubt about it. Reach is a numbers game. Nearly all "mass" media is going to win the reach game.

The problem is, many business marketers stop measuring (or thinking) after they hear the reach numbers. That's an issue. Because let's face it, not all of those people are prospects. Not even a little bit. You are likely reaching lots of people that are not really prospects at all. And more importantly the study shows that not everyone is listening!

RECALL: Not to be crass, but really who gives a crap about how many people you have reached if no one remembers! So now let's dig into the numbers about how the advertising media fare when it comes to recall.

TV Ad Snapshot: 6 out of 10 respondents remembered the company/brand being promoted in the ad.

Print Ad Snapshot: 55% of the respondents remembered the company/brand being promoted in the ad.

Online Ad Snapshot: 31.3% of respondents remembered the company/brand advertised in the ad.

Promotional Product: 82.6% of participants remembered the company/brand advertised with promotional product.

Okay...so in this study we can honestly say that the actual "recall" of the ad is better for the promotional products campaign. Great! Recall IS important. But as I mentioned earlier, the magic is in making people act.

And that's where the real magic happens.

REACTION: You have spent advertising dollars. You want the phone to ring, the mouse to click, and the opportunities to open. What creates the most impact? Let's look at this same 2009 study. This is simply based on what happens after...

TV Ad Snapshot: 3.1% of respondents said they reached out to the company after seeing the ad. 7.1% said they purchased from the advertiser after seeing the advertisement.

Print Ad Snapshot: 4.5% of respondents said they reached out to the company after seeing the ad. 13.4% said they purchased from the advertiser after seeing the advertisement.

Online Ad Snapshot: 4.8% of respondents said they reached out to the company after seeing the ad. 4.6% said they purchased from the advertiser after seeing the advertisement.

Promotional Product: 14.7% of respondents said they reached out to the company after seeing the ad. 20.9% said they purchased from the advertiser after seeing the advertisement.

So let's take this all as a snapshot. What does this mean to you? Well if I were you, I would want potential customers to remember my ad, and react to it. I am a numbers guy so I am going to point something out you. The number of respondents that said they picked up the phone and reached out the advertisers was 3 TIMES HIGHER with promotional products than with these other forms of advertising! That is a HUGE number people!

So as I mentioned at the beginning of the chapter, this is not an indictment of other media. But in so many areas of the business marketing world, promotional products are dismissed as a "throw away." This kind of thinking is harmful to YOUR business! You need to understand that if you hope to be truly successful in the world of business, you better know your numbers!

And if you are using promotional products to promote your business (wisely), your numbers can be pointing UP!

11

MARKETING JOY WITH CALENDARS

It never ceases to amaze me the number of really smart business people who get a case of the "yeah-buts" when they talk about calendar advertising. They have created all kinds of "yeah-buts" in their mind about why this form of advertising won't work for them. They have many (in their mind) well-reasoned arguments about it too.

Yeah-but...they are wrong.

First things first, let's "say this out loud." Sometimes, in business, we overthink things that are not that complicated. I think maybe calendars might be one of those things. "Saying it out loud" forces you to simplify things and decide if (or if not) they make sense. Let's apply it here. Say this out loud.

- Do I want my customers and prospects to take my basic who-what-where message and hang it on their wall all year long?
  Uh...of course you do!

- Do I want these same customers and prospects to hang my brochure up on their wall all year?
  Sure! That would be ideal for any type of business.

- Do I want to have this sort of exposure (did I mention it was all year?) for the cost of one radio campaign?
  Well-yes!

At its most basic, calendar advertising just makes sense. I call it a "foundational piece of marketing." You are not going to use calendars alone to market your business. But it should be the base from which you build the rest of your marketing campaigns. Make sure you get your message on your clients wall (or desk, or pocket, depending on the calendar you choose) and then build from there.

One final question before I get to some of the "yeah-buts." What is the worst thing that can happen to a calendar that you give to a client? Think about it. In reality, the worst thing that can happen is that your client looks at the calendar and then throws it away.

Right?

Guess what. That is the best thing that can happen to nearly any other form of major advertising! If a customer consumes your radio ad, notices it, and then it goes away, it's done its job! So consider that the next time you tell someone calendars won't work for you.

"Yeah-But" no one uses calendars anymore!

Hogwash. Don't get me wrong there has certainly been a shift to technology for personal calendars. I get it. But studies show that there are printed (that means promotional opportunities) calendars in nearly 80% of homes and 80% of businesses (thanks PPAI). In fact there is more than one. Homes average 3 printed calendars and offices average 2.

As a matter of fact, you hear more and more people getting excited to receive calendars because they believe that "no one" gives out calendars anymore! That presents a real opportunity for business owners to fill a need...and get a boost of advertising.

Here's another "say it out loud" moment. That's right. Many of your customers will be excited to get this "as a gift." This foundational marketing tool will be valued because of its utility and will be looked forward too.

When was the last time you could say that about a cable ad?

"Yeah-But" calendars are expensive.

I totally disagree. It's all relative folks. As I mentioned earlier, done right you can get a year's worth of exposure for the cost of one mass-media campaign. Whether it's with radio, TV or even (to a lesser degree) print, small businesses will spend thousands of dollars on campaigns that come and go in the blink of an eye. But then these same marketers will balk at spending that on a year's worth of exposure *directly in the office of the customer they are trying to reach.* This argument just doesn't make sense.

Now it's worth mentioning there are multiple ways to create a calendar campaign. You can use a stock calendar with great pictures and a basic area for imprint. Or you can create a completely custom calendar with your own pictures and information. Each of these options has real merit...depending on the target you want to reach.

As a rule, stock calendars can be less expensive. So if cost is a real concern for you, this might be a better option. But the cost of custom calendars has come down with digital printing, so you might be surprised with the cost-effectiveness of this option. You simply need to decide what you want to accomplish and then move toward that option. We will discuss that more later.

The basic point is calendar advertising is an extremely cost effective way to promote your business or organization. It is less than pennies per exposure. And I think most importantly, it is not wasted. Your message is reaching directly into the homes, offices, desks and minds of your target market.

"Yeah-But" calendars are passé.

Maybe it's because calendar advertising has been around for 100 years. Maybe it's because some business marketers are always chasing the new "shiny" thing. But sometimes the "yeah-but" comes because they think calendars are an old way to go to market. Maybe you think that.

Remember that "say it out loud" thing? Let's do that again. I want you to say:

"I don't want to use an advertising and marketing tool because it has worked for 100 years for thousands of companies."

Sounds dumb, doesn't it?

Calendar advertising is NOT passé. It is proven. Hundreds of thousands of companies have utilized this tool in the tool box to promote and grow their business. Nothing is around in the business world this long if it doesn't work.

Period.

"Yeah-But" I get lots of calendars and I throw them away.

Congrats! You are super popular. But here's the thing; you are the exception. Many people actually go to the mall during the holiday season and buy themselves a calendar. If that is your client, you just missed a huge opportunity.

The other problem with that argument is this you might throw a few away, but most people keep their favorite. So the issue is not that you get too many calendars. The issue is you get too few that move your excitement meter. I always tell people that the cost of a calendar is not determined at the point of purchase. It's determined at the point of hanging. If you spend $.50 each on 1000 crappy calendars and only 1 of them is put on a wall, then that was one damn expensive calendar.

The rule is the same for mugs, mouse pads and calendars. Yes, most people have one. But if you give them one they like better, they will use yours. So don't always go cheap on the calendar. It might be a very expensive mistake.

So now I have addressed just a few of the "yeah-buts." You either believe me or you don't. My guess is, if you are still reading, you do! So let's talk about some options for calendars...and which might make sense for you.

STOCK CALENDARS

There are tons of shapes and sizes and themes when it comes to "stock" calendars. Basically a stock calendar is simply a calendar that is mass-produced that has a specific space for you to put your business information on. Some examples of stock calendars include:

Appointment Style Wall Calendars: These wall calendars are the most popular style of promotional calendar. They often come with pictures ranging from scenic to puppies and kittens to motivation and thousands of others. These can be a great inexpensive way to reach customers in their home or cubicle.

Executive Style Wall Calendars: These are generally larger, grander calendars that are meant to be displayed in an executive office or board room.

Year At A Glance Wall Calendars: The name says it all. These calendars show the entire year on one page and are perfect for planning.

Desk Planners: These calendars are used all over the world to plan hair appointments, schedule vacations, and massages. Though some people believe that calendars are only being done on the computer, this type of calendar is still very popular.

Desk Pad: A great calendar to be able to have right on the desk to display appointments.

And there are lots and lots of other stock styles as well. What you need to do as a business marketer is simply decide where you should best try to reach your customer. Then choose the style of calendar best suited for that location.

A big advantage of a stock calendar is you can purchase a small quantity without breaking the bank. You have less flexibility on what you can put on them. But stock calendars can be extremely effective when done right!

CUSTOM CALENDARS

As the name suggests, a custom calendar can be created from scratch to fulfill any of the above styles...but with your company's pictures, styles, information and more. I always tell my clients that they are starting with a blank piece of paper. So within reason, you can do pretty much whatever you want to do on a custom calendar.

The custom calendar is fantastic because you go from putting your "who-what-where" message on the wall (which is great) to putting your entire company brochure on the wall. You can showcase products, services, case studies, success stories and more. You really have a chance to go all out and "story tell" on a custom calendar.

In addition, though Custom Calendars are generally more expensive than stock calendars, the cost has really come down. So reach out to your promotional consultant before you dismiss the idea of creating a custom calendar. It might be more in your budget than you think!

What it boils down to is, you should be incorporating calendar advertising into your marketing budget. Create a calendar campaign that you can be excited about and then build the rest of your advertising the rest of the year on top of it. Once you create the solid "foundation" you will find a great year can be built with ease!

12

COMBING #PROMO WITH #SOCIAL=#SUPERPROMO

The fact of the matter is, smart marketers combine their advertising and marketing efforts all the time. I talk with business owners and marketers that talk about making sure their "branding is consistent" across the platforms of TV, Radio and Print. That's great! The problem is, they often tend to leave out Social and Promo when they consider their marketing platforms.

The other reason I like to combine these two is for another reason. Both Social Media and Promotional Products are often discounted as advertising media that "don't work." It's even funnier to me to see that both of these advertising venues are discounted for the opposite reasons. Social is too new (for some people) and Promo is too old.

As you might have guessed, I don't subscribe to the theory that either of these advertising platforms "don't work." They both do (quite well actually) if you know what you are doing.

As Social Media guru and superhero Gary Vaynerchuk says, "Just because you can't shoot a three pointer doesn't mean your basketball is broken." Some people who are marketing with Social and Promo are throwing stuff out there without "spending any time in the gym." (I just wanted to keep the sports metaphor going!).

GIVE FIRST STRATEGIES

One reason I think Social Media and Promotional Products are great allies is they are both most effective when utilized in a "give first" strategy. As Gary points out in his book

"Jab, Jab, Jab, Right Hook" a business that wants to be successful on Social Media needs to be willing to spend some time to develop credibility first. They need to add value by sharing information, humor, insight, and engagement (Jabs) to their audience. Only after doing this for a period of time does the business earn the right to effectively ask for the sale (Right Hook).

The same is often true with the very best promotional product campaigns! The very best promotional campaigns are often built around branded products that are functional. They are valued! Although they are marketing tools for sure, when they are done right they are often perceived as gifts to the potential customer. The business marketer "gives first" to provide value. Then they have the chance to ask for the sale!

TARGETED AND NATIVE

Successful marketers on Social Media are wise on telling their story in the native tongue of the Social Platform they are using. Facebook, Twitter, Youtube and Pinterest (just to name a few) each are different and distinct platforms. You need to communicate on these platforms "natively" or you have the real opportunity to turn people off. However, if you do speak "natively" and hit the mark with your message, you have the chance to make a big impact.

Similarly, you have the same challenge and opportunity with Promotional Products. When done right, you can reach right into the homes, offices and lives of your exact target market. But if you don't give real thought to where and when your promotional products will be used, you might miss the mark before you even have the chance to tell your story!

PUMP UP POSTS

So if both formats are "give first" formats, I suggest you get them to work together. When working with your social format, you certainly provide value by sharing appropriate articles, fun pictures, and informational videos. Those are great. But what about simply sharing the opportunity for branded swag? What about this on your next Facebook post? Take a picture of a staff member holding a cold beverage in a branded Coolie. Then post:

"We will send a FREE Drink Coolie to the first 100 people to comment on this post!"

That is a great way to provide value AND it nearly ensures customer engagement! Yes, you will incur some cost on a promotion like this. But you create a great deal of buzz within your audience AND likely increase your audience for the next time you want to try to make a sale. Oh, and you have created a great bond with the customer (or future customer) and given them a lasting token to remember you by.

People still by from people (and brands) that they like. Don't let anyone tell you different.

AFFECTING HUMAN BEHAVIOR

Marketing has been, and still is, about influencing human behavior, right? That is where combing promotional and social really can create some magic. Last year, at Hasseman Marketing, we stumbled across a strategy that helped us increase our social presence...nearly by accident.

In promoting "Promotional Products Work Week" we decided to increase awareness through our Facebook page. We wanted to promote the idea of how Promotional Products can help in business (sound familiar?) AND increase our presence. So we quite simply (and crudely) posted a picture of a staff member (Dustin) in our office holding a cute stuffed puppy (with a branded handkerchief around its neck). We said "We are having a contest today! For a chance to win this puppy you need to do three things: 1) Like our page, 2) Share this picture and 3) like or comment on the picture.

Wow. The results were amazing. That one post is still one of the largest number of impressions we have ever received on

Facebook (with no ad bucks spent) AND we increased the number of likes on our page by 40%.

No you can't do this sort of thing all of the time. Yes it could be obnoxious. But the results were incredible. It just goes to show you, promo affects human behavior!

So work to provide value to your clients in both the Social Media world and the Promotional realm. It will pay off! But if you can combine them, you can Super Charge the effect!

Go get it!

COMMONSKU CASE STUDY

Here is a great case study that combines the use of a custom stress piece (the Commonsku mascot) and Social Media. It also combines two great companies within our industry: Jetline and Commonsku. This fun promotional piece infiltrated our own industry with pictures of the....well...wait. Let's hear it from Commonsku founder Mark Graham!

Consider this. Ultimately, Commonsku is an end user if you consider that we are a software company that has used promotional products as part of its go to market strategy. Given my background in the industry, I leveraged the power of promotional products to help generate buzz and awareness as well as to reward and recognize our customers and prospects. Bigger picture, we have used promotional products to create an emotional connection between our brand and the people who use our product.

When we created our mascot skubot, we knew that he could come alive in several different ways using promotional products. One such way was through a custom stress toy. I have never been a stress toy guy as I felt they are quick to get thrown out, but I recognized that a custom stress toy in the shape of a character that was cute and approachable was a different story. Enter Jetline.

Dana and I worked together for almost a year to create this campaign around skubot stress toys. We were looking to drive two business goals: to generate awareness and buzz for Commonsku as well as educate people about the possibilities around custom stress (a relatively new and unknown part of Jetline's business).

To support the campaign, Commonsku designed a few web properties.

http://commonsku.com/bringingstressback/ was meant to drive sign ups for one of the stress skubots. Jetline sent these out in a nice package along with a case study card inside.

http://commonsku.com/therealcasestudy/ was meant to educate distributors (and end users) about how custom stress toys are made from beginning to end.

http://vimeo.com/74113721 was the stop motion video we created to create that emotional bond between our customers and the company. It was also meant to showcase that stress toys aren't landfill and that they can actually be coveted.

At the end of the day, the campaign was a massive success. Both companies handed out 2500 of these bots. They drove conversations and pictures on social media, they heightened awareness for Commonsku, they drove signups and conversions for Commonsku and they educated thousands of distributors on the potential of custom stress as a legit promotional product.

This campaign was a bona fide double whammy. It not only served as a powerful promotional product for an end user (Commonsku) but it also served to educate and inspire distributors on how to sell this particular product line through the sites we created.

13

REACHING CUSTOMERS AND PROSPECTS WHERE THEY ARE!

It's a cold winter evening. The work day is nearly complete. Amy looks out her office window and notices that darkness has already set in. These shorter days sometimes drag her mood down and make her temper as short as the sunshine.

But the day is not done for Amy yet. She has yet to make her decision on what interior decorator she is going to use in her new office. Her new law practice is doing well, but Amy wants to make sure that the image she wants to portray is carried through the entire facility. Oh, and she wants to like the environment too. After all, she is going to spend most of her waking hours here for the next several years!

Amy takes a deep breath and sets her folder aside. There are several decorators to consider and they all come highly recommended.

She looks to her left and sees lovely calendar that XYZ Decorations dropped off last week. It's sat on her desk ever since. Amy thumbs through the months and sees different designs, from different locations on each month.

"Wow. XYZ has some great designs," she says to no one in particular. "In offices and homes...they seem to nail it. Maybe I am making this too hard."

Amy reaches for her phone and calls to discuss her project with XYZ.

And they live happily ever after!

The cynics in the room will be saying "Yeah, sure! If it were only that easy!" But here's the thing folks...sometimes it is.

Promotional products are a fantastic advertising medium to reach customers and prospects right where they make their purchasing decisions! If you have a product where these decisions are made in the office, you can tailor make your campaign to reach into offices. Are the purchasing decisions for your organization made in the home, kitchen, garage, etc.? Figure out where you want to reach your prospects or customers and then create your items to reach them there!

Let's use the office as the place that your customers are most likely to make their purchasing decisions. There is some VERY valuable real estate you may want to own in that area! In the example above, Amy decided based on a custom calendar that showcased XYZ's fantastic design. So the decorator (who was obviously targeting office design jobs) created a lovely calendar (essentially a hanging brochure for her) that captured valuable office real estate on prospects' walls.

What about that desk? There are some very logical places to gain valuable "desk space." You could create a really cool looking mouse pad. "But everyone already has a mouse pad," you might say. And you might be right. But I have found that if you give someone a better or cooler (or just newer mouse pad) they will often use yours.

Not into calendars and mouse pads? I might disagree, but okay! What about pen holders, desk calendars, notecubes, scratch pads, sticky note holders, letter openers, coasters, tape dispensers, staplers, or clocks? Not enough ideas? Keep looking around your desk and see what invaluable item you can't seem to live without. My guess is, you can do that as a promotional item with great effectiveness.

You get the idea. You need to spend time envisioning what your perfect clients office might look like...then give them a promotional item they will love to keep!

14

DELIVERING MARKETING JOY...AT YOUR OFFICE

If you really want to create "Marketing Joy" to your customers and prospects, you need to create a great customers experience. Your customer needs to not just "endure" their experience with you. They need to "delight" in it. The ultimate goal is to know that when they see your face (or email, or phone number, etc.) they smile! That smile comes from knowing that you (and your company) will provide a pleasant experience from beginning to end.

Here's the secret: That experience can't just come from you. You HAVE to create a team in your company that specializes in customer delight...and it needs to be the whole team. If your sales experience is wonderful, but when there is a problem, your team drops the ball, the whole company blew it. We know this from the customer experience. Often we can really tell the well-intentioned company by how they handle a problem!

I tell the team at Hasseman Marketing this all the time! Everyone can look like superstar when everything goes right! It's when there is a problem that we have a REAL chance to separate ourselves from our competition.

"Great," you say. "But how do I create an internal team that buys into the customer experience like I do?" Great question! There are three key steps, I think:

First, you need to provide clear direction to what you want... and what is important. You have to set the expectation clearly and concisely. Leadership 101, right?

Second, you need to remind them regularly and "show" them with your actions. Leadership 102?

Third, (and most pertinent to this book) you need to create a HAPPY and SAFE work environment!

Workers within any organization, company or team operate best when they feel a level of comfort, contentment and safety. If you want to provide a customer experience that exceeds expectations consistently, you need a team that believes in the mission, feels safe to act on it, and feels appreciated in their efforts.

So let's dig into this just a bit.

SAFETY AT WORK

This might seem most basic, but it's important nonetheless. If you work in an environment where safety is a concern, like a manufacturing facility, safety at work is not just a "feeling." Your most basic job as a leader is to make sure your team goes home to their loved ones every night. There is no more important job! The best way to ensure that you have a safe work environment is to show, each day, that safety is job one. As a leader you can do this in quite a few ways.

First, by making sure there are safety standards in place for each procedure that takes place. There are lots of books in place to help you with that. Second, make sure you follow the procedures yourself! If you expect your team to wear safety glasses, then lead by example. It's as simple as that.

Another way to focus on safety is to create a program that rewards safe work. By simply having these programs in place, you show your team that you have their safety in mind ALL the time. It also shows them (money talks right?) that you have made a financial commitment to put your money where your mouth this! There are lots of forms this might take. But a safety program shows a real commitment to safety that can show big dividends.

And here's the best news! Your safety program can also SAVE you money as well! Check out the case study at the end of this chapter to see how!

SHOWING APPRECIATION

Once you move the basic notion of keeping workers safe, your goal should be to keep team members focused and happy! Happy workers are much more likely to help you create the customer experience you want.

Why? I think its basic human psychology.

If your team feels un-appreciated, un-safe or un-happy, they will be spending a great deal of their energy "protecting themselves." This energy might be channeled into making sure they get credit for work, bringing down others, complaining, or simply looking for another job! All of that time will NOT be directed to making your customers get a great experience.

And oh by the way, if you do lose team members, how hard is that on the team (and the customer experience)? Studies show that replacing a team member costs 1 ½ times more to the business based on training, time off, interviewing, etc. Let's face it; replacing a good team member is a real pain!

So what can we do to make sure the team feels appreciated? There are lots of ways to make your team feel appreciated. And frankly, there is no "right" way to do it. But the good news is, your team members are no different than your customers! They do want to be valued...so the concepts are the same. Let's start with just a few here!

Tell Them About It: To quote Billy Joel, you need to "Tell Them About It!" Make sure you take the time to sincerely (and that is the key word here) tell them how much you appreciate them...and the effort they are putting in. I find that focusing on their effort is important here. Why? Because when you focus too much on the successful implementation of the task at hand, you can make your team fear making mistakes. You want them to know you love the effort. That will give them the freedom to try new things... and feel safe to do so!

Greeting Cards: You may want to dismiss this as old school (and it is) but sending your team members the occasional "thank you" card will absolutely make them feel special! I do this every now and then for our team. I don't want it to be a scheduled thing because then they might come to expect it. The magic is when they open their mail to find a sincere note from me...out of the blue! "Thanks for being a part of the team...and making it a better place!" It's a simple, but wildly powerful, message.

Service Awards: What does this mean? Quite simply, it means you create a program that makes a public display of appreciation for their time served on your team. It can be a certificate, a watch, a ring, etc. But it creates a lasting bond that reminds them why they like working for you in the first place!

Oh...and for those that say, "My employees just want cash." No they don't. More and more studies are showing that cash is LESS valuable than a real gift and show of appreciation. Cash will be spent on groceries and gas. The idea of something like this is to create a positive memory every time the employee looks at the gift. That creates real long term value! I don't mind the idea of including cash if you want... but it shouldn't be the only thing!

Incentive Awards: The concept is very similar here as with Service Awards. You want to give your team a reason to strive. Cash might be a part of it, but the most powerful gifts are more than that. I remember vividly when my wife and I were recognized as Sales Leaders of the Year for an Industry company back in 2004. We received a watch and were brought up in front of the group. I still wear that watch and remember that day fondly! It's about creating lasting bonds and memories like that with your team!

Team Day Out: Take just one day out of the office as a team together and do something fun. We will take a day each year and head to a restaurant and head out on the lake on a boat. We usually try to do some sort of team building exercise in order to get to know each other better as well. Each company culture is different. But we find this is a fun way to get tighter as a group.

Merit Awards: Now for those of you that say, "We have a service award program, we are good." Not so fast my friend! Remember, it's more than just saying "Thanks for sticking around!" A 2012 study by Bersin & Associates show that companies that have effective recognition programs have 31% lower voluntary turnover. That's a big number. So it's not JUST about saying "you've been here 10 years, thanks." That's good. But make sure you are taking the time to appreciate any time it's appropriate. It goes a long way!

As I said, there is not a specific "right" way to create this kind of culture. But there is a real connection to a good team... and how they treat your customers. So you need to consider bringing "joy" to your team if you hope for them to Deliver Joy!

SAFETY CASE STUDY

As promised, we have a case study below that shows how a great safety program can not only make a company safer, but it can help the bottom line as well!

Company Name - Glazing Saddles, LLC

Campaign Type - Employee Incentive Programs

Promotional Keywords -   Motivating Employees
Promoting Safety Programs
Encouraging Attendance/
Involvement
Educating Employees or Customers

Objective
To develop a safety incentive program to motivate employees to prioritize safety in their work environments in order to reduce the incidence of employee and/or customer accidents or injury and to ultimately decrease the number of insurance claims and overall premium costs for the company.

Strategy Execution
When significant safety issues were identified within the organization, our challenge was to develop a customized safety incentive program that would motivate both in-store employees and delivery driver employees to consistently participate in the program to insure maximum results. With two separate groups of employees with separate safety issues, a premium award incentive program was chosen due to its versatility. The strategy behind the logo and theme RISE TO THE TOP was to make a connection with the "rising dough" of the doughnuts the employees make, sell and deliver; and the desired "rising safety" in the organization. Full-color posters were created and posted in the store break rooms for a daily reminder of the program. The colorful, fun graphics incorporate the Glazing Saddles "doughnut hole"

character and summarizes the program goals. It also includes photographs of some of the top awards available to entice the employees to participate. Travel tumblers and lunch coolers have been used in conjunction with the program launch and interim promotion of the program. These specific items were chosen based on the high probability that the employees would actually use the products in their day-to-day work environments and/or at home. The clear acrylic travel tumbler has a full color digital paper insert within the walls of the tumbler depicting the RISE TO THE TOP logo and program goals. This item was handed out during the kickoff meetings for the launch and inserted in the tumblers were the specific rules for either a driver or an in-store employee. The lunch coolers were distributed by the store managers as a motivational piece a few months into the program to help keep the program and the importance of safety "top of mind" with the employees. Since the driver employee group poses the biggest liability due to potential traffic accidents, they can earn monthly points individually or quarterly awards within their driver teams. Safety goals for drivers include zero traffic accidents, zero traffic violations, protecting company issued equipment, attending monthly safe driver meetings and passing a company safe driver quiz with 90% or higher. The in-store employee group safety goals revolve around preventing employee and/or customer accidents in the stores. To maximize the excitement for in-store employees, a scratch card game program was developed where store managers award 30 employees per month of which 14 are Instant Win Scratch Cards offering a variety of awards. The back of the scratch cards were printed with specific categories of positive behavior including: identifying a safety hazard, going above and beyond performing a safe action or something as simple as wearing a big smile or being a team player. The cards were filled out by the manager with employee name, store location, and which behavior was recognized. The manager sends all the cards to the corporate office monthly where they are logged into a back-end system and there is a monthly drawing for all winners to win an extra 20,000 points. In addition, if any store Team completes a calendar month with zero accidents, each employee in that store is awarded another 1,000 points. Safety Points are awarded for pre-determined safety "goals" (behaviors) and are redeemed through the custom branded RISE TO THE TOP Incentive Program web store. Secure logins are given to employees so they can redeem their awards, check point balances or review safety goals. The back end programming allows management to monitor points awarded and redeemed and generate reports participation, store participation along with safety goals that were reached.

Results

In the words of our client, this program is a "true success story!" Within the first eight months of the program launch, the number of insurance claims decreased 56% and the dollar value of the claims decreased by 91%. The biggest surprise came when Glazing Saddles renewed its insurance and its premiums were reduced by $40,000 – which was more than the cost of the safety incentive program. The program has been so successful Glazing Saddles is currently looking at tying in additional components to the program such as customer service, tenure, and an increased sales component. Last but not least, the word of success has spread quickly to other Krispy Kreme franchises and several have expressed interest in adopting the program within their organizations as well.

15

FUNDRAISING AND NON-PROFITS WITH PROMO

There is a large group of people hovering anxiously around a painted line in the road. There is an electric energy in the air as they look at their watches. Some of the participants are stretching and kicking their legs in order to get ready. There is a shout from the front of the group

"Runners! On your mark! Get Set!"

Then a shot rings out and the group of runners dash away from the start line in a group of controlled chaos. There are fast runners, slow runners, walkers and weekend warriors. All of them have come to challenge themselves at this latest 5K. And all of them will be raising money for a cause.

There are thousands of ways that organizations raise money to increase funds and awareness. Local 5K races are popping up everywhere. Why? Mainly because they are (relatively) easy to plan and there is potential for funds for the organization. (It doesn't hurt that the organization can promote healthy living AND increase awareness as well!).

And there is one thing that all of these 5K's have in common. It's all about the SWAG! Usually it's the race t-shirt that runners covet. But it could be the race bag, race medal or all of the above. Runners want to challenge themselves to see how fast they can run. And they want to do it in a group for socialization and recognition. But don't kid yourself. They want the race shirt.

The lesson here is that (when done right) promotional products can have a BIG impact on your organizations next fundraiser.

The concepts on how promotional products can affect a fundraiser are similar to how they can affect behavior for a business. But just to get your creative juices flowing, let's discuss a few here.

INCREASING DONATIONS

One way I have seen non-profits successfully use promotional gifts to help in fundraisers is to incentivize higher giving. The organization will create "gift levels" that inspire donors to give a little bit more to get the nicer gift. Obviously, if you are going to employ this tactic, you need to have promotional incentives that move the meter! The key is to focus on things that have really high perceived value, without breaking the bank! But you can see this technique successfully used by everyone from Big Brothers/Big Sisters at Bowl For Kids' Sake to your Public Radio and TV.

When creating a program like this, value is very important, but so is exclusivity. If you can create a promotional gift that is a "one of a kind" then you have a great chance at really affecting behavior! If you want donors to really step up their donation, then you better step up your game. Think outside of the box here!

What about a custom "letterman's jacket" that is done in the organizational colors?

What about a custom guitar?

Think of an "award" type promo that can be considered a collectors gift, but can also promote your organization for years to come.

The lesson is, if you want a big result then make sure you are thinking big with your items!

INCREASING PARTICIPANTS

At the end of the day, you want as many people involved with your fundraiser as possible. One of the best ways to increase your membership is to offer an incentive to "sign up." As an example, my team and I are helping a local mud run to increase racers and ultimately, increase donations to our local park. The race itself has been going on for two years and is well-respected for the course and the obstacles. Now we just need to increase the number of racers!

So the first thing we did was to improve the quality of the race day t-shirt. Many 5K races (and other local races) default to a basic cotton t-shirt for their race day giveaway. And for certain races, that is fine. The problem is, most serious runners don't wear a basic cotton t-shirt when they are running. They want a nicer "performance" t-shirt. So by improving the basic t-shirt element, you not only increase the likelihood they will wear the shirt later (and promote your event) but the shirt also becomes a reason to do your race, rather than another. As a runner, I know this is a part of the discussion when choosing a race.

The other thing we wanted to do was incentivize early sign up. Having racers signed up earlier has several advantages. You can better plan for everything from water stations to parking to even that t-shirt order. In addition, you get money in earlier to fund your promotional efforts. So this year we are giving away a basic drawstring backpack for the first 250 racers that sign up. This has quickly increased early sign ups and helped us promote the event overall!

PROMOTION OF THE CAUSE

Of course the long term effect of these promotions is you also get to promote your organization or cause! At the end of the day, the reason you are raising money in the first place is so you can do the most good! By promoting your organization (long term) you not only increase your reach, but you also make fundraising in the future easier and easier. Why? Because donors are more likely to give if they know and understand the mission and impact of your organization.

So whether you are planning a local 5K to raise $1000 or a huge capital campaign with the intent of raising $1 million, make sure you consider the impact of including promotional gifts in the mix.

PROMO AS A FUNDRAISER

But before I close this chapter, I would be remise if I didn't mention the idea of creating a custom promotional item and then selling it to raise money. In this case, of course, you would be using the promotional item as the fundraiser itself. You see this sort of fundraiser all over from booster clubs selling t-shirts and sweatshirts to cheerleaders selling sunglasses. The opportunity to provide your "community" (whatever that means for your organization) a custom, valued piece and raise money in the process.

Here are some pieces of advice when using this strategy (and it's a good one):

Think Perceived Value: If you want to sell something for a good profit, you need to buy something that has a high-perceived value. In other words, try to buy something for $5 that you can sell for $12! This may seem like common sense, but a lot of non-profits get items that are "cool" in their eyes but don't make them any money. Get something you can mark up!

Be Different: I mentioned t-shirts above. That's a great item because of the perceived value think I mentioned. The challenge is everyone is doing t-shirts. But don't worry. You can make yours different by doing performance t-shirts or creating a very cool design.

Think Outside the Norm: This obviously relates to the point directly above. But the point is, think about products that are different. If you want to stand out, do a product that not every other group is selling! You will stand out and be able to charge more. And isn't creating revenue for your organization what this is really all about?

CASE STUDY FOR RAISING MONEY WITH PROMO

There are thousands of ways to use promotional products to create a fundraiser. I am going to give you just two that might be a little outside of the norm.

Reason Around Your Wrist

An elementary school needed to create a fundraiser with a quick turn around. The goal was to raise $1500 in two weeks. So they armed their sales people (the students and teachers) with information to take pre-orders for a customizable bracelet. The bracelet is customized by printing a picture and putting it on the bracelet. You can find more information about these bracelets at www.formyreason.com.

The students went out and sold these for $5 to family and friends. They raised over $1600 in that short period of time to go to scholarships! Quick and easy...great stuff.

Creating at Community Calendar

I have seen this fundraiser done for many organizations and it has been a big hit! It can also create a year in, year out source of funds and pride in the organization or community! It takes a little more elbow grease but you can make some real money.

The concept starts with a 12-month custom calendar. One each page you focus on a specific community business or attraction that can be photographed (is already has been) beautifully. Most communities have lots of these pictures already! Each page on the calendar will focus on a different cool photo from around the community.

Now create a committee to sell a sponsor for each page of the calendar. The amount you need for sponsors varies by how many you print. For this discussion you will print 1000 calendars.

Let's assume the complete custom calendar costs $5 to print. You have $5000 in cost to cover. So each page sponsor would cost between $400 and $425 per page. This is very affordable considering there will be 1000 of these circulated for the business owner! Now the entire cost of the calendar is covered.

Now sell the calendars for $10 (or more) and you have a fundraiser that has serious gusto! Oh, and you have a community promotion piece that everyone can be proud of. Way to go!

16

P90X3 AND PROMO

THE POWER TO CHANGE PEOPLE

For those that are unaware, P90X3 (and the preceding franchise) is an intense fitness program from Beachbody. The promise the program makes (and keeps) is that if you do this routine each day for 90 days, you will make impressive changes in your fitness level. The before and after pictures they show in their info-mercials and online are powerful motivators.

The goal of P90X3 (and any fitness program) is to help people change their own behavior, right? In order for any fitness program to succeed, you need to start the program, and then consistently do it day in and day out. They want to modify human behavior. I don't think it's any wonder why they have partnered with promotional products to make it happen.

Let's start with how it has been marketed thus far.

THE POWER OF THE HAT

Beachbody has a network of "coaches" that help them market their product (No I am not a coach. I have no affiliation with Beachbody). These coaches also help with motivation and support (and to sell additional Beachbody products). Before the initial launch of the product, Beachbody promoted P90X to their coaches to build hype. They shared testimonials from test group participants and videos from the creator Tony Horton. Then they shared that if you ordered from a coach, you received an extra workout and a P90X3 hat!

I think there is really sound reasoning to this strategy. P90X3 is an extreme program. It's tough. Especially at the beginning, it is really easy to say "screw this it's too hard!" By setting each person up with a coach, each person has a little support system that will help them "keep pushing play." The goal is to change behavior...so the support group can help you do that! By adding this small incentive, Beachbody is driving people toward a behavior that is in the participant's best interest. In addition, those wearing that hat have proudly announced that they are using this new program (thus promoting it!).

INSIDE THE PACKAGE

When you receive the package you will of course find the DVD's with the workouts. There are quite a few discs, including one you need to watch to "get you ready." They also include an extensive workbook with descriptions of the workouts and a diet plan.

In addition, you will find a sheet of stickers to put on your phone, laptop or tablet. Love it.

Why does this matter? Again it plays into the psychology that by putting this sticker on a device you have committed. People will ask you about that sticker! How is that workout? Is it working? Is it tough? It's a subtle reminder that you have to do the work outs to be in the club.

BEFORE AND AFTER

The final thing I noticed was full page sheet showing two great looking, fit people wearing the P90X3 t-shirt! Do I want one? Of course I do! Heck I sell t-shirts and I still want that t-shirt! What do I need to do? Just take my before and after pictures and send them in to Beachbody!

You see, one of the best marketing tools Beachbody has for programs like P90X3 is the before and after pictures. They can talk about increased health, lower cholesterol, etc. all day long. But if they can show people they will look better in a bathing suit—bam!—now they have your interest!

So they are using the P90X3 t-shirt to remind me (and incentivize me) to take before and after pictures and give them new marketing material for their program!

An extreme fitness program is ALL about modifying human behavior. So I don't think it's any surprise that a smart company is helping people make healthy changes (and increase their sales along the way) by using promotional products to make it happen!

17

SUCCEEDING IN THE GIVE FIRST ECONOMY
(Bonus Chapter of Delivering Marketing Joy)

> *"The person that gives the value first has the leverage."*
> ### *- Gary Vaynerchuk*

We are living in a "Give First" economy. That is my belief. I believe that the person, salesperson, entrepreneur or company that has the strength to provide value first, will win...long term.

The Give First economy does NOT mean the good old boys network. It does not mean that just because we play golf together you have to buy from me. It's about value. It's about providing more than you are paid for. It's about doing business "the right way."

Push vs. Pull: Why? Because times have changed! Since the beginning of marketing and advertising, we have lived in a "push" world. The company that pushed their message out the strongest and the loudest won. But with the onset of the internet (and social media) that has changed. Consumers have the ability to tune us out. They have the ability to shut us off. The power in the relationship has changed.

So we need to pull customers in. We need to "give first."

> *"Life is an echo. What you put out you get back. What you give you get."*
> ### *- Zig Ziglar*

But here is the great news, when it comes to Promotional Products: this plays right into what our media does so well. Our business is built on the idea that we provide something of value first, so that we might be able to earn your business. This is great for the professionals of promo...and those who understand how to tap into its power.

"Okay," you might be thinking, "I believe you. I need to give first. But what does that mean?" Great question. We are going to dig into some real things you can start to do today in order to impact your business. But be forewarned, these are going to seem like common sense. They will seem simple. But here is a very important secret: simple is not the same as easy.

"The greatest distance in the world is the distance between "I know" and "I do."

So let's dig into the steps for building a business that succeeds in the Give First Economy.

Give Joy: That's right. Give out Joy. The world needs more of it. Studies will tell you that 89% of everything you see in the world is negative. With social media and the culture today, my guess is that number should be higher. We are a culture that is drowning in the negative. That's the bad news. But the good news is, it's pretty simple to stand out. Just be positive. Give out Joy. By being the person that spreads good into the world, you have the ability to not only stand out...but to be the kind of person someone WANTS to be around.

You will be different. And in the mind of the customer, better is not better...different is better.

> *Pro-Tip: Do an audit of your personal social media pages. Look at the last 10 posts. If 4 or more can be "perceived" as negative, then you are likely seen as negative. Be on the lookout for ways to push out joy!*

Give Praise and Thanks: Here's a scary statistic: 69% of customers that leave you will do so because of perceived indifference. They will leave because they don't think you care. Yikes. But you can do something about that. Take the time to send real thank you notes. Stop by when you are not selling something just to say thanks. Be grateful for your clients business. You be pleasantly surprised by the response.

Pro-Tip: The best organizations and sales professionals send thank you cards. Most don't. If you are not, start there. If you have mastered that, gather your client's birthdays. Send them a birthday card...they will not be expecting that!

Give More Than They Pay For: Seth Godin says that if you want to be remarkable, you need do something worth remarking about! This is a simple, but totally under-used way to make people appreciate and remember you. Simply provide more value than your customer is expecting. When you do this, consistently, your customers will find you remarkable.

Pro-Tip: The next time you have a large order of polo shirts, add in a jacket embroidered with the companies logo in it. If you are smart, you make it in the size of the buyer. Maybe this becomes a future sale...maybe not. But you will have provided more than they paid for...and that WILL pay off.

Give Content: Though we are going to spend an entire segment on this, it's an important piece of the Give First success plan. Social media and content (creation and curation) are great tools to use to provide value up front to customers and prospects.

What does this look like? It might be as simple as sharing an article that would be helpful to your client base. It might be a fun video about your staff. It might be pictures of your team having fun. There are tons of ways that content can help you provide your customers and prospects value.

What it is not is selling first. Too many entrepreneurs, sales professionals and organizations try and use social media to "push" their message out. You have likely seen them. They simply say "buy from me, buy from me, buy from me" and never provide value.

Pro-Tip: Think of ways to tell your story and provide value through content. Though we dig deeper in this later, start thinking of they way you are most comfortable. Are you a writer? Do you like to take pictures? Are you a talker? Think about what you most enjoy...and get ready to provide value there.

The fact is, there are tons of ways to win in the Give First Economy. The best news is, we are in an industry that is perfectly suited to leverage it. But what about the most obvious?

Give Promotional Premiums: It may seem obvious at this point, but this entire book is about "giving first," and how to do it right. Succeeding in the Give First economy begins and ends with a strong promotional campaign. It is the essence of giving first.

Pro-Tip: Create a monthly SWAG promotion for you and your company. Select them based on the time of year and your customer base. Then order them 3 months at a time (and have them shipped around the first of the month). When the new box comes, you know it is time to get out and "give first" to your clients.

18

A CLOSING THOUGHT ON DELIVERING MARKETING JOY

As I pointed out at the very beginning of this book, "The times they are a changing." I believe we are in the middle of a shift where customers not only want more from brands... they are demanding it. We are flocking to do business with companies that actually provide value in addition to the transaction. That "value" might be as simple as a smile at the counter, a fun picture on Facebook or Twitter, or Thank You card in the mail. But customers (and we know this because WE are the customers) want to be valued and appreciated.

Customers are looking for companies that "Give First."

The great news is, as I have documented relentlessly throughout this book, Promotional Products can provide a PERFECT way for your company to provide value and long-term marketing power to your customers...and your brand. Promotional Products have been a "give first" media for over 100 years!

No matter what business you are in, or what kind of organization you run, there is a promotional product solution that can help you grow. I am sincerely confident of that.

Thank you for taking the time to read this. I hope you get the opportunity to "Deliver Marketing Joy" to your customers and prospects!

If you want ideas on Delivering Marketing Joy, you can always contact me on Twitter @kirbyhasseman. Please feel free to find me and reach out.

And if you want to learn more about this great industry (nearly $18 billion at this point) here is a cool website to check out: http://www.promotionalproductswork.org/. This website from PPAI has more Case Studies, ideas on how to create a plan and even the history of the industry.

So to end this journey, I want to quote Dr. Suess.

> *"You have brains in your head. You have feet in your shoes. You can steer yourself in any direction you choose. You're on your own, and you know what you know. And you are the guy who'll decide where to go."*

It's time for you to go Deliver Marketing Joy! Only you can decide how you will do it!

PRODUCTS SPOTLIGHTED IN CHAPTER 4

Safety Flashlight
http://us.starline.com/catalog/product/16757

Travel Mug
http://us.starline.com/catalog/product/32789

Cooler Bag
http://sevillegear.com/product-details/12-Can%20Convertible%20Duffel%20Cooler/7/0

Barbecue Set
http://us.starline.com/catalog/product/1278

Calendar
http://norwood.com/product/3211/Motivations/

Tumbler
http://www.goldbondinc.com/tubehc

49586848R00064

Made in the USA
Middletown, DE
20 October 2017